The Everything
Pet Rabbit Handbook

Your Ultimate Guide to Pet Rabbit Ownership, Training
and Care.

By Sarah Martin

Copyright © 2014 Sarah Martin

ISBN-13:
978-1495488597

ISBN-10:
1495488594

Sarah Martin

All inquiries should be addressed to:

Sarah Martin

POB 1127 #A1104

Quartzsite, AZ 85346-1127

USA

www.EverythingRabbit.com

This book is a product of the United States of America.

The information and advice in this book is for educational purposes only. All matters regarding health and wellness should be supervised by a licensed veterinary specialist.

Table of Contents

STOP HERE!

Please check out our companion website at

www.EverythingRabbit.com

-   For Your Free Downloads   -

Included with your book are plans for building a mini rabbit transport cage, monthly health checklist (do this before you buy a rabbit!) and a chores checklist.

You can also sign up for our newsletter, find answers to all your rabbit questions & connect with others in the bunny community.

Please visit us and help support our quest to deliver great rabbit information!

A portion of our proceeds go towards supporting free rabbit education and 4-H clubs.

Thank you for purchasing our book. Please leave a review on Amazon so that we can make our future revisions even better!

Introduction

Welcome, my friend, to the wonderful world of rabbits and rabbit ownership!

If you are looking for a crash course on all the basic bunny knowledge you'll need to own a rabbit, then you've come to right place!

In this book you'll find chapters covering everything you need to know including:

- Do rabbits make good pets?
- How to choose a rabbit.
- Health checks to go over before purchasing.
- Recommended rabbit breeds.
- Where to find and buy a rabbit.
- Equipment, food, and nutrition.
- Handling and bunny body language.
- Litter box training.
- Grooming and care.
- Vet visits and what you can do to increase the life of your pet.

And so much more!

This book is your first step towards responsible and enjoyable pet ownership – so congratulations!

Don't forget to get your free downloads that come with this book at www.EverythingRabbit.com. You'll find plans to make your own mini rabbit carrying cage, a health checklist (which is a must before buying a rabbit) and a chores check list.

Have fun and enjoy learning about the wonderful world of bunnies...

Chapter 1:

Do Rabbits Make Good Pets?

Rabbits have been kept as pets since the Victorian era and have been loved by many owners as a playful and quirky companion. In this chapter we'll explore some of the history of pet rabbits, look at what you can expect if you decide to get a pet rabbit and answer the question, "Is a rabbit a good pet for me?"

Rabbits as Pets

A Quick History

Almost all of the pet rabbits that you see today are descendants of wild European rabbits. Keeping and raising rabbits goes all the way back in history to the Romans (the same people who brought you indoor plumbing, concrete, and namesake for the Caesar salad). During Roman times, rabbits were raised for their meat and fur in large, walled in bunny cages called colonies, but it wasn't until much later in history that people would start to breed rabbits for pets and for show.

Cue the 19th century. In-between the invention of the steam locomotive and American settlers heading out in wagon trains across the USA, groups of people, mostly in Western Europe and the United States, start breeding rabbits for show and exhibition. By the time the Victorian era came around, rabbits had become a common household pet.

In 1910 the American Rabbit Breeders Association is founded and rabbits are solidified in their status as more than just a farm animal. Now people all over the world are breeding, raising, and showing rabbits just for fun and enjoyment.

Fast forward to today and rabbits are the fourth most popular pet in North America - right behind dogs, cats and fish. Rabbits are the third most popular pet in the United Kingdom.

Bunnies have become so popular that they now have

their own specialty websites, toys and even trainers (have you ever met a professional rabbit trainer?). Millions of families all over the world enjoy companionship and love from their pet rabbits.

Interesting Bunny Facts

- A rabbit's teeth never stop growing and they manage to fit twenty eight teeth inside that tiny mouth.

- Most domestic rabbits will live to be about five to eight years old, but the oldest living rabbit in recorded history was sixteen years old (crazy-old in rabbit years).

- A bunny is a very athletic animal and can jump up to 36 inches high and run as fast as thirty to forty miles per hour! Try and keep up with that speed Mr. Coyote!

- Rabbits come in all shapes and sizes, from the smallest breed (called a Netherland Dwarf) weighing in at barely two pounds to GIANT breeds of rabbits that can match the girth of most medium-sized dogs. The biggest recorded rabbit is named Darius who weighs in at a monster-sized fifty pounds!

Rabbit Companionship

Rabbits are lovely companion animals and are very social in nature. In the wild they usually live in small to medium-sized groups called colonies. Pet rabbits still need that same companionship and connection that their wild cousins have, but that is where you (the rabbit owner) get to build a relationship with your bunny.

What Can I Expect from My Pet Rabbit?

A pet rabbit, just like a person, will have a personality and attitude uniquely their own. Many people who haven't had a pet rabbit before think that a rabbit will not be as interactive as, say, a dog or a cat, but that couldn't be further from the truth. Rabbits, being the naturally social critter that they are, can enjoy playing and cuddling with you as much as you'll enjoy it with them.

What is a rabbit's personality like?

Rabbits are a "crepuscular" animal, which means that they tend to be the most active at the beginning of the day and at the end of the day, perfect for most households since our days tend to be scheduled that way too. It also means you will have lots of quality time to interact with your bunny when they are in their most playful state.

Each and every rabbit will have their own unique personality. Different breeds tend to have certain personality traits so it's important to "get to know" a rabbit before you decide that you'll be a good fit together.

Are you an active person who loves to be outside? Then a bunny that is spunky and inquisitive could be a great personality match for you.

Do you prefer to sit on the couch and watch a movie or read? Then a mellow easy-going rabbit that likes to cuddle could be a perfect fit.

It's important to observe any rabbit that you are thinking of owning as a pet and assess for yourself whether their individual personality will mesh well with you and your lifestyle.

What is a rabbit's normal lifespan?

Most domestic rabbits will live five to eight years but can live well beyond that when they are kept in good health and have quality care. Depending on the age of the rabbit you bring home, that means that you're looking at having a companion for many years to come - so be sure that you are ready for that kind of commitment.

Won't a rabbit want to eat everything? Can I really have one in my house?

It's an interesting fact that a rabbit's teeth never stop growing and they constantly need to chew on things to keep their teeth the proper length, but that doesn't mean that your pet rabbit will munch his way through your coffee table.

Rabbits make great house pets and, with the right prep work, you can easily rabbit-proof your house before you bring home your new pet (we'll talk about that in Chapter 6: What Should I Do When I Bring My Bunny Home).

There are also a variety of rabbit treats and toys to keep your furry friend busy and active so that they stay away from Grandma's antique dining room set.

Is a Rabbit the Right Pet for Me?

Choosing to get a pet, any pet, is a big decision and shouldn't be taken lightly. All pets require time, energy, money and an emotional investment from their owner. Ask yourself these questions, and be honest, to help you decide if a rabbit would be a good pet for you.

Do I have any allergies?

If you're allergic to rabbits, dander, dust, or to hay (and

there is a lot of hay involved with bunnies), then keeping a pet rabbit might not be a good choice for you.

If you're not sure whether you are allergic to any of the items listed above, then you can have a test done at an Allergist's or Immunologist's office (they're special allergy doctors). Another option is to spend some time with rabbits before you commit to having one as a pet. You can do this by visiting a local rabbit breeder or going to a rabbit show in your area.

Do I have the time to take care of a rabbit?

Rabbits are very loving creatures and will need interactive social time with you and exercise time to keep them happy and healthy. You'll also need time for cage cleaning, grooming, feeding, and all the other responsibilities that come with owning a pet.

Be truthful with yourself and look at the free time you have right now. Could you spend an hour or two a day with your new bunny or do you barely have five minutes to spare as it is?

A pet shouldn't be a burden to an already over-stretched, over-stressed life. If you think that you do have the time to devote to a bunny, then keep reading to see if you can also answer positive to the rest of these questions.

Do I have the space?

Lucky for us rabbits come in all shapes and sizes, from teeny tiny to massive, but even a small rabbit will need a space to call their own.

Be sure that you have enough space in your house to devote entirely to a rabbit cage (the bigger the better). A rabbit cage can range in size from only a few square feet to massive, multi-level bunny condos. If you live in a studio apartment and space is already at a premium, you may not be able to give up any to a big ol' rabbit cage.

Rabbits also like to live away from loud noises and things that might disturb them so keep that in mind when looking for a place for a rabbit in your house.

Am I willing to commit for five to eight years?

A rabbit, with proper care and feeding, will live for five to eight years and beyond. Are you ready to devote that much of your life to having a pet?

Pet ownership can be a very rewarding experience but shouldn't be jumped into without thought for the future.

If you're a stable person who is ready for a bunny-

lifetime commitment, then a pet rabbit could bring you joy and companionship for years and years.

Are my kids ready and responsible enough to have a pet?

A household with kids can be a great environment for a rabbit or it could be less than ideal if the kids are not ready and able to work with a pet bunny.

Children need to be shown how to handle and play with a rabbit safely. They will also need adult supervision with a rabbit's needs and care, even if the bunny is "their responsibility".

Rabbits also do have sharp teeth and nails so kids will need to be taught how to work with a rabbit properly for the safety of both the bunny and the child.

If you're not sure if your kids are ready for a pet, then don't test it out on a pet rabbit. There are already shelters overrun with unwanted bunnies.

If you and you're kids are ready though, then be prepared to be converted rabbit lovers for life!

So... do you think that a pet rabbit might be a great pet for you? Have you read through this chapter and are still excited to learn more? Then keep reading as we explore all the equipment you'll need before you bring home your new bunny. We'll also talk about how to choose a rabbit that can become your ideal pet.

Sarah Martin

Chapter 2:

What Kind of Cage and Equipment do I Need?

Rabbit equipment is very simple, straight forward, and not super-expensive (yeah!). In fact, if you're a handy person you can make a lot of it yourself.

There are a few basic items that you'll need to keep your rabbit happy and comfortable and a few other things that are just for fun - toys and treats all around!

Start with a Rabbit Cage

Every bunny needs a place to call home, but with so many choices out there, what kind of cage should you get?

Rabbit cages (also called a rabbit hutch) range from modest, square studio apartments to huge, multi-level bunny mansions. The grandness of the living space is really up to you (and your budget), but there are a few things to think about before purchasing a cage.

Something to look for in a bunny cage is one that has a door on the top of the cage and on the side. Most cages only have a door on the side, but I've found it is much easier for new rabbit parents to lift their rabbits out if the cage has a top door (just something to think about as you start shopping for cages).

Here is a quick overview of the different rabbit cage construction styles available and the pros/ cons with each style.

Rabbit Cage Types

All-wire cages: These cages are made with galvanized wire (sometimes with a coating) and will have either a

wire floor or a direct floor (meaning that your rabbit will sit in the bedding at the bottom of their cage).

These cages are my favorite style because they are SO EASY to clean. All you need is a sponge and some bleach water and BAM, the cage is sterilized.

I also like that you can take these cages outside and hose them off, if needed. Since there is no wood or other porous material you won't be doing any damage to the cage.

Another major perk of wire cages - your rabbit can not eat them! So you won't have holes or chewed spots like you'll end up with on plastic or wood cages.

Whether you get a cage with a wire bottom or a direct bottom is up to you.

Perks of the wire bottom cage is that all the droppings and urine will "fall through" the wire onto a catch tray underneath so your rabbit is never sitting in wet soiled bedding. They also won't be digging in the bedding that's in the tray so it will keep the space around the cage from looking like rabbit bedding exploded all around it (some rabbits LOVE to dig and can make quite a mess in the process).

Cages that have a direct floor are great for bigger rabbits (a wire floor can stress their feet) and breeds that have short rex fur which can cause their feet to rub and get sore on a wire floor. Some owners also like letting their rabbits have a place to dig and snuggle into their bedding.

If your cage has a wire floor, you can always add a box filled with bedding and hay just for digging.

You can also easily attach urine guards to wire cages. If you get a male rabbit that isn't fixed and tries to spray urine everywhere, you will want to get side-guards on your cage to help keep everything in. These are just short (usually 3-4 inches tall) angled metal strips that can be placed around the bottom edge of the cage so that your rabbit's urine stays inside.

I'd recommend that you order these online since urine guards can be hard to find in pet stores. Or, even better, look for a cage that already comes with them installed!

Wire Cage Pros:

- o Relatively cheap and easy to find (available at most pet store mega-marts AND at your local feed stores).
- o Super easy to keep clean.

- If you're a "handy" person, you can make a cage yourself.

- Rabbit won't chew through metal.

Wire Cage Cons:

- May need extra side guards to keep urine in the cage.

- Galvanized metal will rust if moisture is left in direct contact with it so must be kept relatively dry.

- Wire floors can be harsh on large or Rex-fur breeds (because the fur on their feet is very short) so you will want to purchase a direct floor cage.

The photo on the next page is an all-wire cage that was sold as a kit. Kits can be a great way to get all your rabbit essentials covered at a discounted price than if you bought each item separately.

Wire and plastic cages: A combo of wire and plastic, these cages are usually built with a wire cage frame and a plastic bottom tray that the cage frame sits in. These cages may also have plastic doors.

Warning: If your thinking of getting a cage with plastic parts, make sure that your rabbit can not reach those plastic parts with their teeth. If they can, YOUR RABBIT WILL CHEW ON THEM, which you don't really want (not good for the cage, not good for the rabbit).

That said, if the cage only has a plastic bottom, then it can be an ideal rabbit habitat. A wire frame means that your rabbit can't chew on it and it's still simple to keep clean. This is a great combo with a deep plastic tub-style bottom, which will keep bedding and urine in the cage.

You will have to put a little more effort into keeping the plastic bottom clean (vs. metal), but a bonus is that it won't rust like a metal bottom eventually would.

Plastic can absorb odors though, so make sure you keep a good cleaning schedule for your bunny's cages.

Wire and Plastic Cage Pros:

- o Easy to find (available at most pet store mega-marts).
- o If the plastic tray has tall sides, it will keep all the bunny stuff (bedding, food, urine, etc) in with the bunny.
- o Bottom won't rust.

Wire and Plastic Cage Cons:

- o If any plastic is in a place that can be chewed, it will be.
- o Plastic can absorb odors so will need to be cleaned regularly and replaced if it gets stinky.

Wire and wood cages: These are the traditional rabbit cages that most people will see on farms and in homesteading magazines. Usually, these cages consist of wood frames/wood roofs with wire sides and a wire bottom.

I have seen some beautiful wood and wire cages for sale online and at pet stores that are designed to look like mini house, tiny barns and all sorts of other cute bunny-sized architectural structures.

They are a popular choice for people who keep rabbits outside because the cages usually have a wire floor that is open to the ground so you can rake and sweep away the poo instead of lining a cage bottom with bedding.

These cages are also fairly easy to make yourself If you have any basic tools and handy-man skills.

The wood component is the biggest downside for these cages because (A) your rabbit can and will chew on it and (B) wood absorbs all sorts of things so you can never keep these cages sparkling clean. Wood will also break down over the years (as all natural materials do) and will need regular maintenance and repairs, but this cage design has been around for many years and some rabbit people just LOVE the look and feel of wood/wire cages (they do have a homey feel to them).

I, personally, am not a huge fan because I don't like the upkeep of wood (it wears out) or the fact that I can't keep the cage super clean without serious effort, but if you're willing to put in the extra time, then feel free to check out this cage design.

A quick note of caution:

Make sure that whatever wood is used in your rabbit's cage hasn't been treated with any type of chemical and that its safe for small animal consumption (no nasty chemicals for you bunny!).

Wire and Wood Cage Pros:

- o   Look and feel nice.
- o   Come in outrageous and fantastic designs.

Wire and Wood Cage Cons:

- o   Hard to clean/ will absorb odors.
- o   Can be expensive.
- o   Your rabbit will chew on the wood.

Plastic cages: All-plastic cages are usually sold for hamster or guinea pig owners. There are some that could be big enough to hold a rabbit, but that doesn't mean you should get one.

A plastic cage will be eaten (and all that plastic will, hopefully, pass through your rabbit) and these cages seldom have enough ventilation to keep your rabbit happy.

These cages also tend to get scratched/ broken easily and can be difficult to keep smelling clean (remember, plastic will absorb odors).

I would recommend going with one of the other cage styles for your rabbit – skip the plastic, you'll be happier with another cage and so will your bunny.

Plastic Cage Pros:

- o Cheap.
- o Easy to find.

Plastic Cage Cons:

- o They will be eaten.
- o Poor ventilation.

- o Easily broken.

- o Hard to clean.

- o Can be too small to comfortably hold a rabbit.

Alternative cage ideas: Now that you have a basic understand of what a "typical" rabbit cage looks like, you can let your mind wander into the possibilities of other things that could be re-purposed into a rabbit cage.

I've seen galvanized metal livestock barrels turned into lovely rabbit homes by just adding bedding to the bottoms and multi-level platforms so the rabbit could climb and roam.

Your imagination is all that limits you so, if you like to build things, think outside the box and you could create your own bunny house.

Cage Size: How big does my rabbit's cage need to be?

You rabbit will love to have room to roam so go ahead and get them the biggest cage you can that will still fit your budget and the space you have available.

Actual size requirements posted by the American Rabbit Breeders Association say that, depending on your rabbit's weight, there is a minimum size cage you should purchase. Remember this is full grown, adult body weight so if your rabbit is still young you may need to upgrade to a larger size in the future.

Rabbit Weight – Cage Size:

- Less than 4.5 pounds – minimum cage size is 1.5 square feet.

- 4.5 to 9 pounds – minimum cage size is 3 square feet.

- 9 to 12 pounds – minimum cage size is 4 square feet.

- Over 12 pounds – minimum cage size is 5 square feet.

I think that these sizes are a little small and always like to give my bunnies extra space so they can play and exercise.

For the height of the cage (from the floor to the ceiling), it should be a minimum of fourteen inches tall, taller if you have a big rabbit (over 12 pounds).

Whatever cage you get just make sure that it's easy for you to keep clean and safe. Also remember that bigger is better so check the over-all size to ensure that your cage is big enough for your new furry friend.

Cage Accessories and Other Fun Things

Feeders (for pellets)

Rabbit feeders range from simple crock-style ceramic dishes to metal trays that hang on the outside of the cage and project into the cage (so you don't have to open the cage to feed your rabbit - you just scoop the food into the hopper and it rolls into your rabbit's cage).

Whatever feed container you choose, make sure it has these important features:

1. Can be secured to the cage wall so it can't be tipped over. Usually food containers are secured either by wire, a clamp, or a hanger built into the design of the feeder.

    Your rabbit will enjoy playing with whatever he can find in his cage, which will include his food bowl if it's not attached to something. Having a un-attached food bowl means that any rabbit food in the bowl will be thrown to the bottom of the cage and wasted.

2. Must be big enough to hold all his food (see chapter 3 on feeding for details) but not so big

that your rabbit could sit inside the bowl, which would only get messy.

Rabbits are very clean by nature and can learn to use a litter box quickly. If your food bowl is big enough for your rabbit to sit in, he may decide that it's a good place to go to the bathroom. This is not very clean or healthy so should be avoided.

3. Be made of a material that can't be eaten. Metal or ceramic works well, plastic... not so much. Plastic bowls will have to be replaced after your bunny has chomped his way through them.

Check this out too:

A bonus feature of some feeders is that they have a mesh bottom (or wire bottom) so any food dust can fall through, keeping only pellets in the actual food container.

My favorite style of food container is an all-metal hanging-style feeder. You (the owner) have access to fill the container from outside the cage and then the food is funneled inside (for your rabbit).

They're easy to find in metal (so no chewing) and often have mesh wire bottoms (so they stay super-clean and free of debris). Since these feeders also attached onto the cage wall your bunny won't be rolling it around and wasting all his food.

Hay Racks

Hay racks also come in various shapes and sizes and are great for holding a serving of hay for your rabbit.

OR you can set the hay in your rabbit's cage and let him munch on it there. If your cage has a wire bottom, then a lot of the hay will fall through so a rack will help decrease waste.

Hay racks do help to keep hay and grasses contained (so they don't get all over the place) and will keep the hay cleaner while it's in the rack.

Keep the same thoughts in mind for these as we talked about for rabbit feeders: non-chewable material (think metal or wire) that can be attached to the cage wall is a must.

Water Containers

There are an amazing variety of water containers available for the new rabbit owner. They range from dishes to cups to fancy little fountains that tinkle out water, but my FAVORITE style is the hanging water bottle.

Hanging water bottles keep your rabbit's water very clean (your rabbit can't sit in it like they can with dish or cup-style water containers) and the bottles don't take up room inside the cage because they hang on the outside.

Make sure you get a big hanging water bottle (no wimpy little hamster-sized bottle please!) that are meant for larger animals like rabbits.

A rabbit will drink, on average, at least a quarter of a cup of water per pound that he or she weighs. So if you have 4 pound rabbit, you need to make sure you provide at least 1 cup of fresh drinking water every day.

Your rabbit may need more water depending on its diet (how much dry food verses fresh food you're feeding) and depending on the weather. The hotter it is, the more water they'll be drinking.

Your Rabbit Needs Water:

If you notice that your rabbit is drinking all its water before you have a chance to fill up the bottle (your doing this every day, right?) then it's time to get a bigger bottle or a second water bottle. You rabbit should never be without water.

Water for your bunny should be fresh every day, so rinse out their bottles and fill it up! If you notice that the water bottles are starting to get some green growth inside them (usually a form of algae caused by sunlight), then a baby bottle scrubber works great for cleaning those out.

Keeping your rabbit's water fresh and clean is very important to your rabbit's over-all health so keep on top of it. Your bunny will thank you!

Cage Bedding

Your rabbit's cage will need to be lined with some type of bedding to absorb urine/ odors and keep your rabbit clean and fresh.

The most popular option for most bunny owners in pine shavings (don't get cedar shavings, the oils are bad for your rabbits), but there are also a whole variety of options available from your local pet or feed store.

There has been much debate as to whether pine shaving cause respiratory health issues or not so I tend to stay away from them and opt instead for natural and organic fibers or pellets.

One of my new favorites is recycled paper bedding because it is super soft and my rabbits seem to love digging into it.

Whatever bedding you choose, make sure that the container says that it's safe for small animals.

Toys

Rabbits love to play with toys so be sure to toss in one or two for them to enjoy. My favorite style rabbit toys are wood blocks or shapes that my bunnies can carry around and chew on.

You can also make these toys yourself out of fruit tree wood that hasn't been treated with any type of chemical. Just cut the wood into small blocks, sand off rough patches and you're good to go!

Many rabbits also enjoy having a tunnel or small place to "escape" to and hide in. You can find grass and wood bunny hideouts at most pet stores or online.

Hand-made Rabbit Toys:
Esty.com and other online retailers are a great source for all natural rabbit toys and treats if you want to get your rabbit something really special.

Grooming Supplies

We'll go over your rabbit's care and grooming in Chapter 7, but as far as grooming equipment goes - here is a quick list to add to your bunny-supply kit:

- Nail Clippers: Human or cat-style (one cost 50 cents at the drug store, one costs $4.00 at the pet store).

- Brush: If your rabbit has long fur, you'll want a long-bristled brush. If your rabbit has short fur, then get yourself a short-bristled brush. We'll go into more detail on brushes in Chapter 7 when we talk about grooming.

o   Unscented Baby Wipes: These are my secret cleaning weapons that I carry all the time. They can wipe down your rabbit, your rabbit's cage, or you – in case of a bunny accident.

So there you have it, your basic list of bunny must-haves before you get your new furry friend. Be sure to have everything set up and ready for your rabbit before you bring him (or her) home for the first time.

Now that we've gone over the stuff you need for your rabbit, let's talk about feeding. You'll want to have food ready too before you bring home your bunny.

Sarah Martin

Chapter 3:

What should I Feed My Rabbit? Beyond the Carrot.

Your pet bunny's wild cousins (rabbits that roam free in nature) spend their days munching on a whole variety of plants and grasses. Rabbits are strictly herbivores, meaning they eat only plants, so your pet rabbit's diet should consist of a good mixture of green things.

Rabbit Pellets

The base for any good rabbit diet starts with pellets. Rabbit pellets are a mixture of hay, grains, and other nutrients compressed into small, bunny-bite sized pieces of food.

Almost all rabbit pellets are formulated to provide all the vitamins and minerals a rabbit needs to grow to and live so these will be the base for our rabbit's main food.

There are several brands of pellets available and, before you decide on which brand to use, review these guideline for choosing pellets:

- o Skip pellets that have little bits of dried fruit and grains mixed in. You'll be able to see them in the bag. It's the stuff that isn't green. This is like the rabbit equivalent of eating fast food for every meal, every day. Those little bits are high in calories and sugar.

  Often a rabbit will like the little bits of snacks SO MUCH that they start throwing the pellets out of their food bowl so they can get to the good stuff. Stick with straight pellet-based food.

o Flip the bag of food over and check the label. You'll want something that has at least 18-20 percent fiber (rabbits need a very high fiber diet) and has about 12-14 percent protein.

If your rabbit is still growing, you can feed them a higher protein food that has about 16 percent, but once they've reach their adult weight, switching to a lower protein content will help keep them from becoming overweight.

o Some of the very best pellets for your rabbit are soft hay or grass based (like timothy hay, oat hay or Bermuda grass) as opposed to an alfalfa base. Read the label to see what kind of hay was used in making the pellets.

Alfalfa is very high in protein and in calories so can lead to weight gain. You may have to check around to several feed and pet stores or shop online to find timothy based pellets.

Timothy hay also has the benefit of being high

in fiber so it's a great choice for your bunny. On a side note, many of the big name rabbit food manufactures use alfalfa as their base so check the bag before you buy.

Once you've selected and purchased a bag of pellets it's time to store that food. Make sure you keep the pellets out of direct sunlight and in a container that keeps bugs and other animals out.

Just be careful that the container isn't completely air tight or the food could collect condensation and become wet and moldy. If this happens, then throw out that food and start over with fresh, dry pellets.

Keep Rabbit Pellets Fresh:
You'll want to keep just enough pellets around to last you 1-2 months, any longer and the nutritional value of the food starts to go down. If it's been over 2 months, it's time to throw it away and start again with fresh food.

How Many Pellets Should I Feed?

When a rabbit is 6 months old or younger I give them all the hay and pellets they can eat. After that you'll want to start cutting back on the amount of food so that your rabbit doesn't start gaining too much weight.

Here is a quick scale for you use:

- o Small breeds, which weigh 2-4 pounds as adults, should be fed approximately 3-4 ounces (by volume) of pellets once per day.

- o Medium breeds, which weigh 4-7 pounds as adults, should be fed approximately 4-5 ounces of pellets once per day.

- o Large breeds, which weigh 7-12 pounds as adults, should be fed approximately 6-8 ounces of pellets once per day.

- o Giant breeds, which weigh over 12 pounds as adults, should be fed approximately 10-12 ounces of pellets once per day, maybe more!

One of the best ways to judge your rabbit's ideal weight is to keep a close eye on them and if they look thin to you (you can really see ribs sticking out), slowly increase the amount of food.

If you start seeing rolls of fat on your rabbit and they start looking particularly thick around the chest and hindquarters (which is at top of their back where their back legs touch the body), then it may be time to cut down on the food and treats.

Your vet will be able to help you determine a healthy

weight for your rabbit if you have any concerns.

Hay and Grasses

All rabbit diets should be a balance of fresh grass hay, greens, and pellets.

If you've bought a hay rack (which we talked about in our equipment section), then you can place you rabbit's daily allotment of hay inside the rack. If you don't have a hay rack, then a small bowl will do or just place the hay on the cage floor but not in the corner that they like to go poo!

> **Hay is a natural for rabbits:**
> Wild rabbits eat a TON OF FRESH GRASSES every day and the high fiber is very helpful for keeping their gut healthy. Your pet rabbit will also benefit from this high fiber diet so keep a supply of fresh hay in their cages every day.
>
> I usually put in a small handful and re-fill once it starts looking low or clean out and replace if the hay gets dirty or wet.

Some of the best hays to feed to your rabbit are grass-based soft hays, such as timothy, Bermuda or oat hay.

These can be found at most pet or feed stores and, if all else fails, you can always order small bales of hay online.

Avoid feeding your rabbit alfalfa hay (unless your bunny is underweight and you are trying to fatten him up).

Alfalfa hay is very rich in calories and also very high in protein so can lead to weight gain in most rabbits. Stick to the grass-style hays listed above for best results.

When it comes to hay, fresher is better. It's also good to check daily that your hay hasn't gotten wet and started to mold or rot – which can happen very quickly if moisture gets into your hay container.

You fresh hay will keep for approximately 2 months, after that it will start to get stale (and your bunny won't enjoy it as much) so throw it away or mix it into your compost bin.

What if I'm allergic to hay?

If you or someone in your family is allergic to grass hays, then compressed mini hay bales of timothy hay (they really do look like itty bitty bunny-sized hay bales) are a great alternative to lose hay.

Your rabbit won't be getting quite as much fiber, but it's definitely a good option to keep dust and allergens down, if that's a problem for you.

Greens and Things

To round out your rabbit's healthy diet you should include a dose of veggies and greens. These help to supplement the dry pellets/hay and add a fresh element that will help keep your rabbit's meals nutritious and well balanced.

Most current rabbit veterinarians agree that fresh greens are a vital and important component to a complete rabbit diet. Feeding greens will keep your rabbit healthier and give them a better chance of living to a ripe, old bunny age with minimal health problems.

Note that you shouldn't start feeding vegetables or greens to your rabbit until they are over 12 weeks old or it may cause gut issues.

Some of my favorite rabbit-approved greens are:

- Parsley

- Green tops off of carrots

- Collard greens

- Wheat grass

- Alfalfa sprouts

- o Dandelions greens and flowers

- o Mustard Greens

- o Spinach

- o Kale

- o Brussels sprouts (at least somebody likes them!)

All should be washed and cleaned before being fed to your bunny and should be free from any chemical fertilizers or pesticides. Organic greens are always a great choice to keep your bunny chemical free.

When feeding your rabbit greens, start with a small amount (think a tablespoon or two) and work your way up. You can feed up to 1/3 cup of greens per pound of body weight.

If you start your rabbit with too many greens at once, it can lead to diarrhea or soft droppings. If you notice this, then back off and feed veggies and greens every other day until your rabbit becomes accustomed to the food and their droppings return to normal.

Note that super watery leafy greens (like iceberg lettuce) are not good choices for rabbit feed. The heavy water content tends to bring on diarrhea and they are usually less nutritious than "dryer" greens like spinach.

Avoid anything too spicy, no radishes or hot peppers. If you think it's spicy, your rabbit will too and it can cause an upset stomach. Also, avoid dense foods like potatoes, grains, nuts, corn and other high calorie items. These can lead to weight gain and an unhealthy bunny, so stick with the salads.

Rabbit Treats

Rabbits have a sweet tooth and LOVE getting treats. I usually skip store bough treats unless they are dried fruit because most of the commercially produced rabbit treats are made up of leftover bits and have almost no nutritional value.

Some of the best treats for your rabbit will be fruit that you already have in your own home. Bunny favorites include:

- ○ Apples
- ○ Bananas
- ○ Pineapple
- ○ Strawberries

- o Pears

- o Peaches

Pineapple also has enzymes that help to break down hairballs in your rabbit's system so if you have a long-haired rabbit, pineapple may be an ideal treat!

Fruit tree sticks also make a great treat for your rabbit and give them something to chew on and play with. Just make sure that the wood hasn't been treated with any chemicals and give it a good scrub before feeding to your bunny.

Feed treats sparsely and in small amounts. A good rule of thumb is every other day and only about a one inch square piece of fruit at a time.

If you notice that you rabbit is getting pudgy and/or stops wanting to eat his normal food in favor of his treats, then cut them down to once or twice a week.

Watch how much your rabbit eats:

Keeping an eye on how much your rabbit eats can also be one of the greatest ways to catch if your rabbit is feeling sick.

One of the first signs of illness in rabbits is a loss of appetite and low energy/listlessness. If you notice any of these symptoms, call your vet for advice.

Now that you know what equipment you need and what to feed your rabbit, let's move on and start talking about what you should look for in purchasing your new bunny.

Chapter 4:

How do I Choose a Pet Bunny Rabbit?

Here comes the exciting part... actually choosing what kind of pet bunny you want and then going in search of your new rabbit!

In this chapter, we'll go over super-practical things like the age and gender you'll want for your rabbit and also go into more fun things like bunny personalities.

This might be one of the most important chapters for you to read because deciding on the "right" rabbit for you will be the biggest step you take towards finding and enjoying your new pet. So let's dive in!

Should I Get a Boy or Girl?

One of the first questions that every new rabbit-to-be owner asks is, "Should I get a boy or a girl rabbit?" Asking rabbit people this question will always get you different answers (some people love male rabbits, others love females) so we'll give you an introduction to both so you can decide for yourself.

Male rabbits:

Also known as "bucks" (technical term for a boy rabbit – yes, just like a deer), male rabbits have the tendency to spray and "mark their territory" with urine if they haven't be neutered. They will also have a strong urge to breed if not fixed so may hump things (pillows, stuffed animals, your foot) in an attempt to mate.

Not all bucks will act this way though and many of my favorite rabbits over the years have been males. One of the easiest ways to eliminate their hormonal tendencies is to have them neutered.

On a slightly different note, in many rabbit breeds the males tend to have larger more broad-shaped heads, whereas the females tend to have more narrow and angular shaped heads (I guess you could call it a more feminine look).

The girls also tend to be a little bit bigger in size than their male counterparts so if you want a particular look for your rabbit, either masculine or feminine, you'll want to take that into account.

In some breeds you really can see the physical difference between the bucks and does to the point that someone familiar with that breed can tell which is which by just looking at the rabbit.

Female rabbits:

A doe (girl rabbit) can be more grumpy and territorial than a male rabbit, especially during certain times of the year when she's in heat.

Rabbits have a very strong urge to reproduce and a female rabbit can get a little twitchy when she wants to mate – even to the point that they will have a false pregnancy and pretend to make a nest.

Some female rabbits will also spray urine to mark their territory, although their aim is not as high as a buck.

Not all female rabbits will exhibit these tendencies though. Some of the sweetest and most gentle pets I've ever had were female rabbits.

Once again, a lot of their raging hormones can be controlled by having your rabbit spayed.

How to tell your rabbit's sex:

When you are purchasing a rabbit it's always nice to be able to tell if your rabbit is a boy or a girl.

I still remember many years ago visiting a family friend and playing with their bunny. When I asked the name of the rabbit they said, "Suzy," and I told them I thought that was a cute but funny name for a boy rabbit.

Everyone in the family just stared at me with a blank look and then told me that they had a girl rabbit (at least that's what the pet store told them when they bought "her"). I didn't have the heart to correct them.

To check the sex of your rabbit, sit in a chair and place the rabbit on your lap, head facing away from you.

Grasp your rabbit under their front feet and gently roll them towards your body so their back is pushing into your tummy.

Using your thumb, gently move the fur away from their genital area (which is right above the tale) and push down into their skin right above their genitals.

This will cause the vulva or penis to become exposed. (see photo for more details)

Male Rabbit

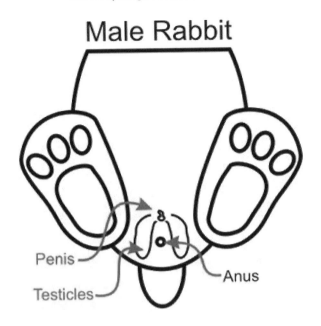

Penis

Testicles

Anus

Female Rabbit

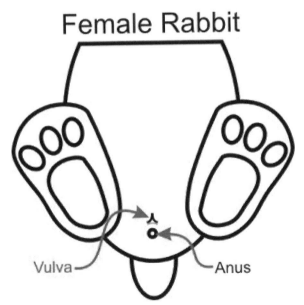

Vulva

Anus

You may want a friend to help you with this if you have both hands occupied with holding your bunny.

Male rabbits that haven't been fixed will also have testicles showing, unless they are really young (in which case the testicles haven't dropped yet).

If in doubt, you can always take your rabbit to a vet and have them tell you the sex.

What Age Rabbit Should I Get?

Average Rabbit Lifespan

Rabbits can live for quite a while (up to ten years or longer) so you'll want to decide what age range to look for in your new rabbit.

Here we will review the different life stages that rabbits go through so you can choose which age is right for you.

Young Rabbits (under five months old)

If you've even seen a picture of a baby rabbit, then you know that they may be the CUTEST creatures in the whole world (no – I think they are definitely the cutest creatures in the world!). In fact, that may be what got you thinking about getting a pet rabbit in the first place.

It's hard to resist a baby rabbit's furry little face or funny antics as they wobble around, still unsure of how to walk with their big feet.

While this sounds adorable (and it is!) there is a slightly darker side to all this cuteness.

Baby rabbits have some of the highest mortality rates of any other rabbit age. With their still-developing immune system they can be vulnerable to illness and disease, so you have to be extra careful about who and what they come in contact with.

Baby rabbits also have a tendency to chew on everything (think puppy here) and don't have full control of their bladder yet, so if you're litter box training they may have a few accidents.

A baby rabbit also won't have fully grown into their personality or body, so you're never entirely certain of what you're getting.

That little half pound rabbit at the pet store might turn into a twelve pound monster even though the gal there told you it was a dwarf breed and wouldn't get much bigger (I've heard that story from many rabbit owners).

You don't know if they'll be quiet, rambunctious, full of energy, or a snuggle bunny – they still need time to come into their personality.

While that might be part of the fun, it's also part of the risk when you start with a baby rabbit.

If you think you can handle it (and be honest with yourself here), then make sure that you get a rabbit that is at least six weeks old. Any younger than six weeks and you risk some serious health problems if they were taken away from their mother too early.

Teenage Rabbits (five months to ten months old)

Ahhh, the teenage years... This is when your rabbit is coming into his hormones (if you haven't had them fixed) and their personality starts to shine through.

This can be an intense phase in your rabbit's life and will usually come with lots of digging, spraying, chewing and urges to mate.

Most of these symptoms will lessen once they get beyond their final growth stage and move into their adult life so it just has to be endured. Know that this too shall pass.

The final size of you rabbit will determine how long the teenage period lasts. Smaller breeds will mature more quickly and may be fully grown after six to eight months. Larger breeds will need a little more time and may take up to ten months to get their adult bodies.

Adult Rabbits (ten months to six years old)

Once your rabbit is fully grown, you'll be able to really get to know the true bunny inside. Here is when their personality will come into full force and their hormones will have settled down.

Adult rabbits are also much easier to train and tend to be less squirrelly or impatient. I guess with age comes wisdom and patience, even for a rabbit.

For families with small children, I always recommend that they get an adult rabbit. Adult rabbits tend to be more mellow and easy going than a younger rabbit.

Mature Rabbits (over six years old)

An older rabbit makes a wonderful companion and pet. They tend to have slowed down a bit and take life at a more leisurely pace, making them a great choice for people who want a quieter bunny (perfect for snuggling on the couch!).

When deciding on which age of rabbit suits you best, make sure that you take into account what you want out of your experience with your pet. You'll have years of fun and love to look forward to, no matter what age you decide to start with.

Personality

Rabbits have as many personalities as people so, although one rabbit might look like another, they could have completely different spirits.

Think about the life you live and the kind of rabbit personality that would match well with you.

Do you like to sit on the couch and read a good book or watch TV? Then you'll match well with a rabbit that is mellow and easy going who can get cozy with you on the sofa.

Are you an active person who wants to go play with

your pet? Then you'd probably opt for a more active bunny that will want to play and explore.

Do you have small children that will be interacting with your bunny? Then you'll want a rabbit that is calm and patient.

One of the easiest ways to decide on a rabbit personality match is to take out a piece of paper and write down your typical day. Now re-write that same day but with a rabbit interacting with the things you do at home.

Where do you see yourself spending time with your bunny? Is it more active or more calm? Start writing down personality traits that you think would fit well with your lifestyle and your own personality.

Rabbits are social animals by nature so love spending time with their group (which will be you!). They will benefit from exercise and daily interaction so picking a good personality fit will help encourage you to spend time with your bunny.

When you go to buy your first rabbit, ask the person you're purchasing the rabbit from about the bunny's traits and personality. Take time to observe the rabbit on its own and how it interacts with you.

As you observe your potential new bunny, look for

signs about what their personality is like.

Are they excited and running around lot? Do they enjoy being held and getting pet? Are they curious about you or would they just prefer to sit and watch?

Really take your time here and try to not get distracted by the bunny's looks or coat color. It's more important for you to find a rabbit that fits with your family than finding an exact color or breed.

It will be very exciting the first time you meet a potential new pet, but stay calm and keep your head about you so you can decide if that rabbit will really be a good fit for your home. If not, then keep looking and don't worry. There's a bunny out there for everyone!

Indoors or Outdoors

You'll have to also think about whether you want an indoor or outdoor rabbit.

Both can be good environments for your bunny, but I think that indoors beats outdoors hands down for many reasons. Keep reading for a quick pros and cons list to both options.

Indoor Pros:

Indoors means that you'll be spending more time with your rabbit (they're a companion in your house) which is great for both you and your bunny.

You will also have a rabbit that lives a longer and healthier life since they won't be exposed to weather swings which cause stress (at the least) and can be a killer if you live in very hot or cold climates.

Wild animals won't have the opportunity to go after your bunny or spread a disease or parasites to your rabbit.

Most people also tend to pay more attention to cleanliness with a rabbit actually living inside their house.

Indoor Cons:

If you have someone living with you who is super allergic or you don't have any space in your house for your rabbit, then you might consider having an outside bunny.

I have known several rabbit owners who keep their bunnies outside and have had years of enjoyment with them. I just think that most people are more attentive to a creature who is living with them (in the house) instead of their backyard.

Outdoor Pros:

One of the pros of an outdoor rabbit is defiantly that you don't have to worry about a mess in the house – which doesn't mean that you won't keep the same cleaning schedule, right?

Another perk of outdoor rabbits is that, as mentioned before, if someone in your house is allergic to hay or pet dander, then you probably can't keep a bunny inside.

If this is the case, really ask yourself if a pet rabbit is right for you since you may not be able to spend the time with your rabbit that it needs.

Outdoor Cons:

One of the biggest cons for me, since I grew up and lived in the Sonoran Desert, is dealing with temperature swings. Certain rabbit breeds deal with hot/cold better than others, but heat can be a killer for your rabbit, literally.

If you live somewhere that gets hot, you'll have to take steps to keep your bunny cool or bring them into the house during extreme temperature spikes. Frozen water bottles work well as cage additions when it gets warm out.

You also leave your rabbit exposed to many hazards when they are housed outside. I've also heard stories of neighborhood dogs getting into people's backyards or wild rabbits passing on fleas or diseases when they came in contact with someone's pet.

The bottom line is if you decide to keep your rabbit outside, be sure to make their space as secure and comfortable as you possibly can.

One or Two Bunnies

Rabbits are very social animals by nature (like us!) so enjoy having members of their own species around... under the right circumstances.

If you are not able to spend a lot of time with your rabbit, then having two rabbits will help them to feel less lonely and will give them someone to play with.

If you're looking for a companion rabbit who will really be your pet, then you will probably just want to start with one bunny. Rabbits that have other rabbits around tend to develop bonds with the other bunnies and less of a bond with the human in their life.

If you do decide to get two rabbits, then remember that two rabbits means twice the work , twice the cage size, twice the food cost, twice the vet bills and twice the time.

Rabbits, while social creatures, also like to have their space (just like us) and have a hierarchy of who is in charge. They will occasionally butt heads with each other just to test and see who the leader of their rabbit community is.

You add raging hormones into that mix and fights can break out that could cause a lot of damage to both of your bunnies. Try to follow the below suggestions to increase your chances of having two rabbits live in peace and enjoy their life together.

I also recommend that people who get two rabbit start them off together at an early age (six to twelve weeks old) and/or buy littermates (baby rabbits who were born in the same litter). You will also want to make sure you get both rabbits spayed or neutered so that fights don't break out.

If you get a male and female rabbit, then you'll also have to be worried about unwanted pregnancy so it's always better to play it safe and have them fixed. Everyone (including you) will be happier in the long run.

If you're trying to introduce two rabbits to each other that have never met before, remember to go slow. Start with just a few minutes of supervised time together in a neutral area (like the living room floor). Bunnies tend to be territorial of their personal space (usually their cage) so this is NOT a good place for introductions. You're just asking for a fight if you take a strange rabbit and place it into another's cage.

It could take weeks or months for your rabbits to get along and some rabbits just never seem to take to each other and may have to be separate permanently.

Purebred or Mutt

Mixed breed rabbit or a purebred, which should you bring home? The answer is - either one - because both can and will make excellent pets. As long as you're not planning on showing or breeding rabbits, then it's really up to you on whether you want a specific breed or a mutt.

With a mutt, you'll be getting a surprise and you will have a very unique rabbit. If you have already fallen in love with a specific breed of rabbit, then do some investigating and see if that rabbit is right for you.

Before you decide on a particular rabbit (purebred or mutt) you'll want to decide what fur type and size of rabbit you want.

We'll start by going over the different fur types...

Rabbit Fur Types:

Rabbits have three major fur types that you'll need to take into consideration – Long fur (also known as wool or Angora fur), short fur or rex fur.

Long Fur:

Long haired rabbits (also known as Angora rabbits or wool rabbits) require regular brushing to keep their coats free of snags and tangles. Some of the breeds with long fur have a very soft-textured coat (like the angora breeds) that mats easily and others have a harsher-textured coat that is easier to keep tangle free (like the American Fuzzy Lop). This fur type tends to be two to four inches long and the rabbits are very fluffy looking.

When they shed their coats (which rabbits do a couple times a year), then you will also have a lot of hair to clean up! If you don't mind putting the extra time in and love the look of long haired rabbits, then consider an Angora breed or a mutt with long fur.

Short Fur:

Short fur rabbits are what most people think of when

they picture a rabbit in their minds. This is the most common fur type out there and most of the rabbits you come across will have short fur.

It's easy to keep clean and groomed so is a good choice for first time rabbit owners or those who don't have a lot of time to devote to grooming.

Rex Fur:

Rex fur is a very short rabbit coat about a half inch long that is super soft and feels almost exactly like velvet (I can hear you saying. "Ohhh!" right now). My very first rabbit was a breed that had rex fur because once I felt how soft the coat was I couldn't see myself with any other type of rabbit.

This coat type is only found on a few breeds so you will need to hunt it down, probably through a local breeder, if you want a rabbit with rex fur. It is the ultimate in softness, let me tell you!

One of the few downsides to rex furred rabbits is that, because their fur is so short, the bottoms of their feet can get raw from rubbing if you have a cage with a wire bottom. If you do have a wire-bottom cage, you'll want to add a "rabbit cage mat" to give your bunny somewhere to sit and keep their feet off the wire. You can order these online or search your local pet store (FYI - I've only every found them online).

Rex fur breeds also can't keep themselves as warm as other rabbits with regular or long fur so aren't a good choice if you're keeping your rabbit outside somewhere that gets really cold.

Rabbit Sizes:

Dwarf, small, medium, large, or GIANT – rabbits come in all shapes and sizes. You just need to decide which size is right for you.

If you have small children, then I would recommend a bigger rabbit as they are less delicate than a dwarf or small rabbit.

The rabbit size you select will also depend on your cage size and space. **If you have a tiny space for your rabbit/rabbit cage, then stay with a smaller bunny (not over five or six pounds).** If you have room and love the idea of a large or giant rabbit (yes – there are GIANT breeds in the rabbit world), then go for it!

Do take into account that giant and large breeds tend to live slightly shorter lives than the smaller breeds, those big bodies just wear out faster.

Rabbit Breeds:

There are over 100 breeds of rabbits worldwide and almost 50 breeds in the USA, the UK also boasts over 50 recognized breeds. You can visit the American Rabbit Breeders Associate website or the British Rabbit Council's website to view pictures of each and every different breed.

There are rabbit breeders and hobbyists all around the world that are constantly working on new breeds and varieties (colors) so there is a wide and vast selection to choose from.

Below is a list of some of my favorite rabbit breeds that also make great pets.

Dwarf Rabbits

- **Netherland Dwarfs** (Max weight is 2.5 pounds)

  These are the smallest rabbit breed in the USA,
  weighing in at about two pounds each. This
  breed also comes in more colors than you can
  shake a stick at. They also happen to be
  adorable with big fat heads that seem too large
  to fit on their bodies. If you want a true dwarf
  rabbit, then look into the Netherland Dwarfs.

- **Dwarf Hotot** (Max weight is 3 pounds)
  Another member of the Dwarf family, this
  breed has an all white body with dark eyes and
  a ring of dark fur around each eye, giving them
  an "I just put on my mascara" look. They have a
  similar body type to the Netherland Dwarf but
  come in only the one color pattern.

Small Rabbit Breeds

○ **Holland Lops** (Max weight is 4 pounds)

One of the rabbit breeds that have lopped ears (so they hang down instead of sticking up), this breed is famous for their rambunctious and clown-like personality. They also come in a ton of different colors and pack a lot of spunk into a small package.

○ **American Fuzzy Lops** (Max weight is 4 pounds) Similar in size to the Holland Lop, this is the only breed of lop-eared rabbit that also has wool instead of regular fur. If you don't mind the extra brushing, then this is an adorable breed of rabbit to own.

○ **Mini Rex** (Max weight is 4.5 pounds)
This is one of the smallest breeds that has a super-soft rex coat and they tend to possess a very sweet disposition. The mini rex also has a nice selection of colors and is a very popular breed so is not hard to find.

○ **Himalayans** (Max weight is 4.5 pounds)

This breed of rabbit has very distinct markings, with an all-white body and colored ears, nose, feet and tail. A calm and happy breed,

Himalayans are one of the best beginner rabbits to own.

- **Mini Satin** (Max weight is 4.75 pounds)
  Due to a genetic quirk, this breed has a super, super shiny coat (the hair shaft is actually translucent so the light reflects off it more than a regular coat). They also have a stocky but compact body that just screams to be cuddled. If you like bling and other shiny things, you will love the look of this breed, they practically sparkle.

Medium Breeds

- ○ **Dutch** (Max weight is 5.5 pounds)

The Dutch is one of the oldest breeds on record and tend to be very gentle animals. The breed currently comes in six different colors, but all of them sport a combo of a dark colored back half with a white chest/ feet. These markings are a trademark to the Dutch breed.

- ○ **Florida White** (Max weight is 6 pounds)
These smaller all-white rabbits are known for a calm and sweet disposition. They also have soft and shiny fur that makes them very loveable.

- **Mini Lop** (Max weight is 6.5 pounds)

  Mini lops are like the mature brother of the Holland lop. They still have the super-cute lopped ears but tend to be calmer and more sedentary.

- **English Angora** (Max weight is 7.5 pounds)
  This is probably one of the most popular angora rabbit breeds and looks like a rabbit exploded fur all over itself – they even have super-furry faces. Their long wool means that they need constant brushing and serious maintenance to keep their coat snag free, but if you're looking for a wooly bunny (maybe you knit and want to

make your own yarn), then this is a great breed option for you.

Large Breeds

- **New Zealand** (Max weight is 12 pounds)
  You've seen this all-white rabbit everywhere!
  When I think of the Easter Bunny, I think of a
  New Zealand. Their white coats always give
  them the look of being clean and polished. This
  breed also tends to be relaxed and easy going.

- **Californian** (Max weight is 10.5 pounds)

This breed has an all-white body with dark markings on their face, ears, tail, and feet that kind of resemble a Siamese cat. One of my favorite breeds, they are big bunnies that are beautiful to look at and to own.

- **English Lop**(Max weight is 10.5 pounds)
  The first time you see this breed of rabbit you'll never forget it. They have the longest ears in the whole rabbit breed world, sometimes reaching over 26 inches from tip to tip (seriously). Their ears will keep growing until about 14 weeks old so you have to keep a constant watch to make sure they don't rip or tear.

- o **Rex** (Max weight is 10.5 pounds)

Similar to mini rex only BIGGER, the rex breed is a popular choice for people who love the soft fur but want a bigger companion rabbit.

Giant Breeds

○ **Flemish Giant** (Max weight – NONE!)

The biggest rabbit breed in the USA is the Flemish Giant with minimum weights in the thirteen to fourteen pound range and maximums going to… BIG. These rabbits are larger than most small dogs and can be about the same size as a medium-weight dog. They have big ol' floppy ears to match with their big ol' bodies and make great companion rabbits… as long as you are prepared to handle a rabbit that size and pay their food bill!

o **Checkered Giant** (Max weight – NONE!)
  This breed is a full on rambunctious breed that
  is high energy and usually very outgoing (be
  prepared!). Not a good fit for everyone, but
  with the right person can be a very fun and
  exciting rabbit to have. They have a white body
  with spots of color running down their sides,
  face, and ears.

Now that you've had an introduction into the world of
rabbit breeds and have been able to think about
personality, size, and age of the rabbit you'd like, let's
talk about where to find that rabbit!

Keep reading and check out our next chapter which
will go over who to buy your rabbit from and how to
find them.

Sarah Martin

Chapter 5:

Where can I get a Pet Rabbit?

Now that you know what you're looking for in a pet rabbit, it's time to go find him! (Or her!) As a rabbit owner-to-be you have a few different options available for locating your ideal pet bunny.

We'll review in this chapter: adopting a rabbit, purchasing from a breeder, and what to watch out for at pet stores or when answering an ad selling rabbits (like on Craigslist).

Shelter or Rescue Organization

Just like cat and dog adoption, rabbits are an often-adopted pet. There are thousands of abandoned rabbits that find their way into shelters and rescue groups every year and need a good, loving home.

It's sad but true that many pet owners don't do their research and don't really stop to consider whether an animal will fit into their lives, but you're not like that, right? You bought this book so you can be a responsible pet owner! **If you want to give back and give an animal a second chance on life, then seriously consider adopting a rabbit.**

Most shelters will ask you to come in and fill out an application and may put you through an interview to make sure you are a good candidate for pet-rabbit ownership. Be patient and compliant with this process. Remember that the employees and volunteers at these organizations are just trying to make sure that you and a rabbit will be a good fit!

You will probably also be required to pay an adoption fee. These fees help to offset the cost of care for your rabbit and the many other animals that come through the shelter's doors. These fees can range from a few dollars to $250 (and up) depending on where you adopt your rabbit and if your rabbit has already been spayed or neutered.

If your rabbit isn't spayed or neutered, then ask the shelter or rescue group for a recommendation for a vet. They often have great insight into who specializes in rabbit care in your area!

You'll find all kinds of rabbits available at shelters and private rescue organizations. There will be mix-breeds and pure breeds. Some shelters may only have a few rabbits to choose from while others (like many of the big private rescue groups) may have 20-100 or more rabbits in their care.

When you go to meet the rabbits and make your selection, be sure to ask if you can take the rabbit to a quite place so you can observe them and get a sense of their personality. Shelters can be a loud and noisy place so you'll want to make the rabbit is as comfortable and calm as possible so their true inner-bunny can shine through.

Talk with the shelter:

Also remember to ask the people working with your potential rabbit what they think the rabbit's personality is like. They often spend several hours a day taking care of them.

After you've had a chance to spend time with your potential new rabbit, you'll want to do a quick health check to make sure they are ready to go to a new home (see the guide and check list at the end of this chapter).

One of the best ways to find a rabbit shelter or rescue group in your area is to do an internet search or check

out the House Rabbit Society's website at
www.rabbit.org and then click on the area you live in
listed on the left-hand side of their webpage (they
keep an excellent list of rabbit rescue resources).

Rabbit Breeder

If you are looking for a specific rabbit breed and color
or you think you might want to show your rabbit, then
you'll probably want to find a rabbit breeder in your
area that specializes in the breed you've selected.

Get to know your rabbit breeders:
Reputable rabbit breeders are an excellent resource
for rabbit knowledge and can be a great acquaintance
to have. It's nice to know you can call someone with
your rabbit questions who has years of experience with
bunnies.

A responsible rabbit breeder will take excellent care of
their animals and ensure that they are kept in top
health. Most of their rabbits are usually well socialized
and handled often, which means the rabbits are very
use to people. Since most rabbit breeders are showing
their rabbits and competing against other breeders,
they will usually have high standards for all animals
that pass in and out of their doors.

Before buying a rabbit from a breeder make sure that you:

- o Ask if you can take a tour of their rabbitry (technical name for the place rabbits are kept). Check to make sure it's clean and well maintained and that all their rabbits look like they are in good health.

- o Ask them to introduce you to the mother and father of the rabbit you're thinking of purchasing. You can usually get a good sense of what your rabbit will look like and what their personality will be like by meeting the parents.

- o Be clear about whether you want a pet rabbit or a show rabbit. Pet rabbits are almost always cheaper and breeders are constantly looking for good homes for their bunnies. Your rabbit may come with show papers and/or a pedigree if you are purchasing from a breeder.

- o Ask the breeder to show you the basics of handling and interacting with your rabbit. They should be very comfortable with holding a rabbit (if they're not, then they may not be as experienced as they tell you) and can be a great resource for knowledge and techniques.

A breeder shouldn't sell you a rabbit that is too young to leave its mother (weaning age is usually 5-8 weeks)

and they should be able to help you make a decisions about what rabbit is right for you.

Make sure you do your homework and find a rabbit breeder who is knowledgeable and is taking great care of their rabbits. If something doesn't feel right, then don't buy from them. There are people out there who claim to be responsible breeders but are just a "puppy mill" of the rabbit world churning out bunnies for profit with no consideration for their health. These rabbits usually have all sorts of mental and physical problems from poor care and inbreeding, which is not something you want to support or deal with.

One of the best places to find rabbit breeders is by going to a rabbit show (then you can also check out a whole bunch of different rabbit breeds at once) or by going onto the American Rabbit Breeders Association's or British Rabbit Council's website (or giving their office a call) and searching for breeders in your area. The American Rabbit Breeders website is: www.ARBA.net, the British Rabbit Council's website is: www.TheBRC.org

Purchasing a rabbit from a breeder can range from inexpensive ($10-20) to very expensive ($50-200) for a specialty color or breed. Almost all rabbits that you get from a breeder will not have been spayed or neutered so take that extra cost into consideration when purchasing your new pet.

Pet Store and Ads

There are many pet stores out there that sell rabbits (and several that don't because of high return rates) so it may seem like a good option, but **make sure you do your research before committing to a rabbit from a pet store or feed store.**

There are some fantastic pet stores and feed stores out there that take excellent care of their rabbits, do quarantines on all new rabbits to make sure they are healthy, and know their rabbit suppliers to ensure they are getting quality bunnies. These types of stores usually offer a health guaranty and have a very knowledgeable staff to help you out.

Unfortunately, this is not typical for MANY pet stores and feed stores so you have to be super cautious when purchasing from these sources. There are many pet stores that keep all their rabbits in one big cage, so unwanted breeding and pregnancy is taking place (can you imagine taking a rabbit home just to have her deliver a litter of baby rabbits a few days later?) and sickness runs rampant.

If you're new to rabbits, it can be hard to tell the good

from the bad, so ask for references from past people who have bought rabbits from that store so you can see if they've had good experiences and, if you even have an inkling of doubt, you'll want to have a vet perform a health check for you before you commit to purchasing any rabbit.

Ads in the paper and on Craigslist should be treated with the same caution. You never quite know what you're getting yourself into, so tread lightly and do your homework.

How to do a Health Check

Before you buy any rabbit you should perform you own health check to make sure the bunny is healthy and ready to come home with you. If in doubt, you can always schedule a health check with your local vet before you purchase any rabbit.

Here we will go through the items you should check over and then give you a quick checklist so you don't forget anything. A copy of the checklist is also available on our website www.EverythingRabbit.com so that you can print and take it with you when you go to look at your new bunny.

First – Observe

One of the first things you want to do is observe your potential rabbit in their cage. If a rabbit doesn't feel good or is in poor health, they tend to hunch in on themselves and huddle into a corner. They may be listless and not very responsive. You want a rabbit that looks healthy and doesn't seem to be suffering in any way.

Second – Interactions with People

Next you are going to take the rabbit out of their cage (or have someone who is familiar with handling rabbits do this) and you're going to see how they interact with you. Is the rabbit aggressive and tries to bite or lunge when taken out? Do they run in terror and look scared to death, even after they've been taken out of their cage and given a few minutes to calm down? These are signs of a rabbit that is not people friendly and may even be a little wild.

Look for a rabbit that exhibits the personality traits that you outlined in our earlier chapter.

Third – Physical Check

Now it's time to get hands on and check your rabbit over for their physical health. You will first run your hands along their body and make sure they don't seem under fed or emaciated. Also check for any lumps or wounds that could be a symptom of some illness or injury.

Now let's look at their fur and run our hands through their coat a few times. A rabbit in good health shouldn't look mangy or be missing patches of fur (no bald spots!). Now, if a rabbit is shedding, they may have some loose fur. This is normal and nothing to be concerned about. This is also a good time to check and make sure they don't have any fleas or ticks on them.

Ears are next on the list. You'll want to check inside each ear canal and make sure there isn't any build up or extreme flaking, which can be a sign of ear mites. Just look into each ear and check it out.

Eyes and nose come next. When a rabbit has a cold, respiratory infection, or a more serious disease like rabbit Pasteurellosis, it will most commonly show up in the form of eye discharge and a runny nose. Check that the rabbit's eyes are clear and bright without any buildup or goo. Also check their nose to make sure it isn't pusy or covered with discharge.

Next we'll be checking their belly, legs and tail - once again searching for any lumps or signs of injury. Just run your hand over the rabbit and feel for anything out of the ordinary.

Once you've complete the basic body check, **look at their toenails.** Rabbits have toenails that continuously grown and so need to be trimmed on a regular basis. If their toenails are not groomed, it can be a sign of poor care.

Check the gender of your rabbit - To do this, take the rabbit while you're sitting in a chair and place them on your lap, head facing away from you.

Grasp your rabbit's shoulders with your left hand and place your right hand between their front legs under their head. Gently roll them towards your body so they're back in pushing into your tummy.

Once they are pressed into your body, remove your left hand from their shoulders, but keep your right hand in place using gentle pressure to keep the rabbit pressed into your torso.

Using your thumb, gently move the fur away from their genital area (which is right above the tale) and push down into their skin right above their genitals. This will cause the vulva or penis to become exposed so you can see which sex your rabbit is (see photo for more details).

Male Rabbit

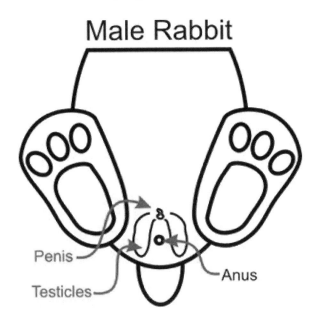

Penis

Testicles

Anus

Female Rabbit

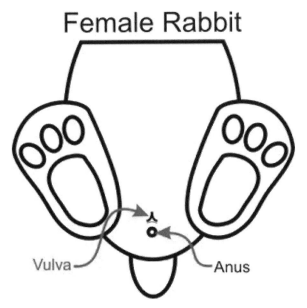

Vulva

Anus

You may want a friend to help you with this if you have both hands occupied with holding your bunny.

Male rabbits that haven't been fixed will also have testicles showing, unless they are really young (in which case the testicles haven't dropped yet).

Along with checking the gender of your rabbit, **you'll also want to check for Vent Disease**, which is a fairly common and very contagious condition in rabbit. Observe their genital area and make sure there are no pimples or pus in or around their private parts.

You will also be checking the genital area to make sure there are no signs of diarrhea or upset bowel movements.

Now here's a tricky one – but SUPER important. **You need to look at your rabbit's teeth.** If you're with a breeder or someone comfortable handling rabbits, you can ask them to do this for you, but if you're doing it yourself, we're going to assume the "check gender" position again with the rabbit pressed against your tummy.

Carefully move your fingers next to your rabbit's lips and move the lips back to expose their front teeth. There should be two big front teeth on top that fit over the bottom teeth.

Upper Teeth
(Over the top of the bottom teeth)

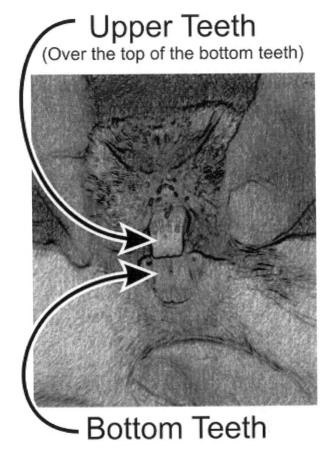

Bottom Teeth

If the rabbit's bottom teeth go over the front OR the teeth meet evenly in the middle, they may have a tooth deformity called Malocclusions that will cause the teeth to wear unevenly and may even make it impossible for the rabbit to eat of not treated correctly.

This genetic condition is very common in breeds that

have large round heads (just not enough room for all those teeth) and can cause a whole bunch of health problems involving eating and diet. Most rabbits with this condition have to have their teeth sanded down weekly just so they can eat (because a rabbit's teeth never stop growing) and rabbits with Malocclusions should never be bred. You don't want to produce more bunnies with this serious problem.

Checklist

- o Observe rabbit in cage - look for signs of sickness and not feeling well.

- o Interactions with people - look for signs of aggression or extreme fear. Have the list of your desired rabbit personality traits available and look for a rabbit that exhibits these.

- o Body, belly, feet, legs, and tail – check for lumps or wounds.

- o Fur – not mangy, no bald spots. Check over for fleas and ticks.

- o Ears – Check for mites/ scaly patches in ear canal.

- o Eye and Nose – Check for signs of discharge.

- o Toenails – You want to see that they are clipped and groomed.

- o Genitals – Check that the gender correct, no discard from genitals or signs of diarrhea.

- o Teeth – Check that your rabbits teeth are aligned correctly (top teeth should be over the front of the bottom teeth).

- o EXTRA: Ask for a small bag of the existing pellets that are being fed to your rabbit so you can slowly change over their food to whatever brand you've purchased (more on this in the next chapter). Make sure you have enough for a week or two.

Use the above information and guide to make sure that you pick out a rabbit that is happy and health.

Here is a copy of the health checklist in a single-page format so that you can take it with you when you check out potential new bunnies. You can also print a copy of this from our website: www.EverythingRabbit.com

Health Checklist

Go through this check list monthly with your rabbit OR any time you are looking at taking home a new rabbit.

DONE? (check off)

O Observe rabbit in cage - look for signs of sickness and not feeling well.

O Body, belly, feet, legs, and tail – check for lumps or wounds.

O Fur – not mangy, no bald spots. Check over for fleas and ticks.

O Ears – Check for mites/ scaly patches in ear canal.

O Eye and Nose – Check for signs of discharge.

O Toenails – You want to see that they are clipped and groomed.

O Genitals – Check that the gender correct, no discard from genitals or signs of diarrhea.

O Teeth – Check that your rabbits teeth are aligned correctly (top teeth should be over the front of the bottom teeth).

O EXTRA - When Purchasing a New Rabbit:
Interactions with people - look for signs of aggression or extreme fear. Have the list of your desired rabbit personality traits available and look for a rabbit that exhibits these.

O Ask for a small bag of the existing pellets that are being fed to your rabbit so you can slowly change over their food to whatever brand you've purchased (more on this in the next chapter). Make sure you have enough for a week or two.

Provided by EverythingRabbit.com, Copyright 2013
This is an excerpt from the book The Everything Pet Rabbit Handbook

Now that you've gotten your new pet rabbit (yah!!!) we're going to talk about what to do when you first bring your rabbit home and how to "bunny-proof" your house.

Chapter 6:

What Should I do After I Bring My Bunny Home?

Yah! Woho! You finally have your new bunny in the car and heading towards home! Time to celebrate; bring out the cake and balloons! But before you go too crazy, let's talk about your bunnies first day in their new home.

Equipment Set Up

Make sure cage is set up and ready. Bedding in the bottom of the cage, water in the water bottle and have the cage placed in the area that it will be permanently staying.

I always like to find a quiet corner where a new rabbit can be comfortable. If you place their cage in an area that's too busy or has constant traffic, it can be too intense for their first week of being in your house. Remember that it can be a scary thing for your rabbit to leave their old home and come to a new one so you want to give them time to adapt.

Your Bunny's First Day

Once you get your rabbit home, place them inside their new cage and let them sniff around. They may be scared at first and just sit there, but give them a few minutes to calm down in their new environment. Their natural bunny curiosity will take over and they will start exploring.

This is the time to be quiet and patient with them. Don't make a lot of noise or have sudden movements, you want your rabbit to think of their new cage as a safe space. Try to sit at eye level with your rabbit and not hover over them. Because rabbits are prey-animals they have a natural tendency to run from things swooping over the top of them. For all they know, you could be a hawk zooming in to get them!

Keep this in mind when interacting with your rabbit, slow movement and try not to "hover" over the top of them until they are accustom to you and feel very comfortable when you're with them.

This first day is all about a calm and relaxing introduction to their new home so keep preliminary intros to other family members at a minimum and make sure that everyone who comes in contact with your rabbit that day walks in with a quiet and patient mind.

It will be very exciting to have your new rabbit in your home, but resist the urge to take them out and play and run around or your rabbit may go into sensory overload and it could take them weeks to settle into their new space.

Think of this first day as a bunny spa and it's your job to create as relaxing and calming an atmosphere as possible. You want your rabbit to enjoy spending time with you and your family and that will happen quickly if they feel comfortable and safe.

Introductions to Your Family

After the first day/ night in their new home, it's usually a good time to introduce your new rabbit to other members of the family.

I always like to use the living room floor for this so that everyone can sit down at bunny level and the rabbit can move around and not feel trapped.

If you have small children, coach them on always being calm with the rabbit so they don't scare them and show kids how to be gentle when petting their new friend.

If you're kids will be handling and grooming your rabbit, then show them how you'd like that to be done so that both your children and the rabbit are safe. This training is usually good to stretch over the course of a couple of days so that everyone gets to practice and feel comfortable before moving onto something new (this includes your rabbit too!).

There will be plenty of time for fun and playing once your rabbit and the members of your family have become accustom to working with each other and feel comfortable.

Swapping Food

Switching your rabbit's pellet food should be done SLOWLY to avoid an upset tummy. Since you got a bag of your rabbit's old food when you picked up your rabbit it will make the transition much easier (It was on the checklist to go over when looking at a new bunny).

For the first two to three days continue feeding your bunny their old food. Its stressful enough to change homes, your rabbit doesn't need the added stress of changing food on top of that.

After the first few days have passed started with small amounts of the new food you've purchased mixed in with the old. Gradually increase the mix of new to old food over the next two weeks until you're feeding almost all the new food OR until you run out of the old.

The idea is to give your rabbit a gradual transition so their stomach can adjust to whatever new blend is in your rabbit food brand (they're all different).

If you try to do this too abruptly, your rabbit could end up with diarrhea and gastrointestinal problems while their gut adjusts.

Bunny-Proofing Your House

If you are going to let your rabbit wander around your house, one of the MOST IMPORTANT things you'll do to ensure they are safe is to take the time to bunny-proof your house.

Now, full bunny proofing will never happen because your rabbit will likely try to take a nibble out of all sorts of things that are within their reach. We're just going to try to remove all the ones that could be potentially harmful to your bunny.

One of the best ways to scope out potential bunny landmines is to get down on your hands and knees so you are at "bunny level" and then take a scoot around your house. Anything that looks like it could be gotten into will be and should be dealt with before you let your rabbit roam free.

Here are just a few of the items you need to watch out for. Remember that your house is unique and there could be many other things that you'll need to move or bunny-proof before giving your rabbit free roaming and never let your rabbit wander unattended.

Power Cords: Your home is full of things that your rabbit would love to (and will!) chew on. Cords need to be moved out of the way, unplugged or barricaded out of reach. A rabbit could be electrocuted if he bit into something that was plugged in.

You can also buy "safety covers" to place over the cords and keep them safe from chewing (Google it and you can find many suppliers).

House Plants: Most of your house plants are VERY poisonous so don't chance it – move the plant out of bunny reach. House plants should always be re-positioned so that your adventurous bunny can't munch on them. It's also safer for your house plants, a determined bunny could eat their way through one in just a couple of minutes.

Furniture, rugs and other brick-a-brack: Wooden furniture and other household items can become a bunny chew toy so keep a bottle of "anti-chew" spray around (like a bitter apple spray) to deter those teeth from munching up your house. This spray is available at most pet stores; make sure you get one that is approved for rabbits.

Most rabbits are very happy to romp and play without being destructive, but keep an eye on them just to be sure they're not gnawing on great-grandma's antique dining room table.

Potential Trap Places: Rabbits like to feel safe so will often squeeze themselves into the tinniest of areas; areas you never thought a rabbit could fit (like your leather boots lying on the floor). They are ground burrowers by nature so it is a normal thing, but that also means you've got to seal off any area that (A) you don't want you bunny to go and (B) that they could get trapped in.

Think of it as a "Where's Waldo" game except with a bunny and roam through your house looking for bad places that could be hazardous if your bunny got into them.

Litter Box Training: To me litter box training is a must for every house rabbit that I've owned (and it is astonishingly easy to teach). We'll go into more details on this in the next chapter, but remember that, even with litter box training, your bunny will have occasional accidents – especially if they are young. Keeping a good pet cleaner handy is always a smart idea to clean up stains and remove odors so your rabbit won't try to use that area again as a poo station.

Next we are going to get into daily rabbit care, grooming, litter box training, and all the other fun stuff that comes with living with a bunny!

Chapter 7:

How to Handle, Socialize, and Grooming Your Rabbit

Along with lots of love and attention, your rabbit will also need to be picked up, moved around, groomed and socialized on a regular basis. Keep reading to find out how to master all of these important skills.

Handling Your Rabbit

It's very important for you, as a new bunny owner, to become comfortable with picking up and handling your rabbit. Proper handling will ensure that your rabbit feels calm and relaxed whenever you go to lift them out of their cage or place them back in. If your rabbit has had a bad experience or has been dropped before, it may take some time to regain trust so go slow and take your time. Slow and steady is how you win this race.

How to Pick Up Your Rabbit

Removing Your Rabbit from Their Cage

Start by placing you hand inside the cage. Don't chase your rabbit around and get them all wound up, this will only add stress to the whole experience. Give your bunny time to calm down before you try to take them out.

You take them out of their cage by placing a hand under their belly and then one hand around their butt (the hand on the butt will support most of their weight).

Lift up with both hands and carry forward towards the cage door to remove them from their cage. Be sure to lift with enough clearance that no rabbit body parts are dragging. Be careful not to drag their toes or nails across the bottom of the cage, this can cause broken toes or nails.

It's very important that your rabbit feels like their back-end is being supported or they may start kicking because they are worried they might fall. Keep both hands securely around your bunny and close together so that your rabbit is not stretched out.

Carrying Your Rabbit

My favorite way to carry a rabbit is like a football (American-style football for any UK or Aussie readers out there).

Once your rabbit has been safely removed from their cage tuck them into the crook of your right elbow (so their face is tucked in between your elbow and the side of your body) and hug them against you. It should look almost the same as a football player who is running with a football – your bunny being the football (the running part is not recommended).

Make sure to try this a few times with your rabbit, lifting them in and out of their cage until you both feel comfortable with the movement.

If you have difficulties getting your rabbit out of his/ her cage, then think about switching to a cage that opens from the top. It's a lot easier to get your rabbit out when you're reaching in from the top and these cages can save you (and your bunny) a lot of stress and chasing.

One way to start rebuilding bunny trust (for a rabbit that doesn't like being taken out of their cage) is to reward your rabbit with a small treat when you take them out and right after you put them back in so that they start associating good things with being picked up and moved around.

If you've had the opportunity to buy a rabbit from an experienced rabbit handler, then ask them to show you their favorite way of moving and holding a rabbit. You can also call your local 4-H extension office and ask to speak to the person in charge of the small animal projects. They can usually direct you to a rabbit 4-H club that will have experienced rabbit handlers. Ask if you can come to one of their meeting and get a lesson on rabbits.

Never, ever try to pick your rabbit up by their ears or any other body part! A rabbit's ears were not meant to support their whole body weight and could cause a broken ear or bone.

Rabbit Body Language

Your rabbit will give you many unspoken signals about how he/she if feeling. Learning to read your rabbit's body language will help you to know what your rabbit's thinking and doing.

Rubbing Chin on Stuff: Rabbits do this to mark their scent on things that they look at as "their stuff". When you first bring your rabbit home or let them wander into a new area they will usually start sniffing around then rubbing to spread their scent (its super-adorable to watch, by the way).

Stretched Out or Laying Around: This is a sign that your bunny is relaxed and comfortable in their environment.

Jumping and Running: When most rabbits feel happy and playful they will run around like little furry madmen and jump high into the air. It's your bunny's way of saying, "Woho!!! I love my life!"

Licking and Snuggling: Rabbit will often bump you (I like to think of it as snuggling) when they want attention and lick you as a way to say, "I love you."

Kicking: Rabbits usually kick or lash out at you if they feel insecure or are worried about being dropped (such as, if you don't have a secure grip on them when you lift them out of their cage). If your rabbit has trust issues from being dropped while carried in the past, be patient and continue to work with your bunny. Once he knows that you will keep him safe and secure he will become calmer.

Stomping Back Feet: Rabbits will stomp their back feet as a warning that something isn't right, that other rabbits need to stay away, or that there may be danger nearby.

Freezing: It's like playing that game that we all did as kids where someone yells, "Freeze!", and everyone stops what they're doing to hold a pose.

Rabbits do the same things, but it's usually in response to a noise or action that has scared them. If you see your rabbit doing this, then try to determine what caused their fear and (if you can) get it under control so that your rabbit doesn't feel afraid. Often rabbits will also flatten themselves close to the ground when they scared to try and make their bodies as small a target as possible.

Shaking Head or Ears: Your rabbit will most often do this when she smells something or eats something that she doesn't like. It's like your rabbit's saying, "Blah! I don't think I like this."

If head or ear shaking becomes a constant thing, then check their ears for signs of damage (mites or injuries could cause an infection) and see your vet if the problem continues.

Hunched Up with Front Feet Held High: Rabbits often adopt this pose right before they try to fend off someone or something by kicking with their front feet. If your rabbit looks like this, he may be nervous and is preparing to fight if he continues to feel threatened.

Biting: Rabbits bite to let you know that they don't like something or when they are scared and afraid. If your rabbit starts nipping at you, he may be saying that he's done and wants to go back to his cage.

Bunnies can also bite when they are feeling aggressive or defending their territory. You can read more about dealing with a rabbit that bites later in this chapter.

Eating Poop: Rabbits don't have a super-complex digestive system like we do so to extract extra nutrients from their food they store it in a special "hindgut" that ferments the food and helps break it down. This results in a specific kind of poo (that's right, rabbits have special poop) that a rabbit then eats to obtain the extra nutrients.

This process is called Coprophagia and is a totally normal part of the rabbit digestive process.

These special pieces of poo (called cecotropes) look smaller and wetter than regular poo and are usually eaten immediately by your rabbit but may sometimes be seen in the cage. Weird, I know, but all part of the rabbit-learning process.

Noises: Your bunny can (and will make) a whole variety of strange and adorable sounds. I had one rabbit that would purr when I pet him (it sounded like my bunny was trying to gurgle water) so keep on giving the love and see if you have a rabbit that purrs!

Most rabbits will grunt when they are unhappy about something and they can also scream (at the top of their lungs) if they get really frightened or feel like they need to sound an alert.

Socializing and Bonding with Your Bunny Rabbit

Most pet owners love to spend time with their animals. It's a great way to de-stress and build a deep bond between owner and bunny. The more time you spend with your rabbit, the greater your bond will be.

Here are some of my favorite ways to bond with my bunny:

- o **Sitting on the Couch**: Whether you're watching TV or chatting with friends, couch sitting is an easy and relaxed way to include your rabbit in your daily life.

- o **Reading a Book**: Most rabbits enjoy their peace and quiet. Let your bunny chill with you as you catch up on your reading.

- o **Fixing Dinner**: While you're cooking away your bunny can play! I like to bring my rabbit into the kitchen to wander and play while I prepare dinner. Anytime I'm fixing dinner with some "bunny approved" greens he always ends up getting an extra snack from me.

  I like to use baby gates to block off the rest of the house when my rabbit is in the kitchen with me. That way, he won't wander and get into trouble.

- o **Yoga**: Floor poses during yoga are usually done slowly and calmly. This can be a fun way to include your rabbit in more of your daily life. Let them hang out with you on your yoga mat while both you and your bunny relax.

- o **Family Game Night**: Let your whole family (including your rabbit) sit around the living room and enjoy each other's company.

- o **Play Time**: Designated play times are a great way to bond and exercise your rabbit. Exercise pens (usually sold for small dogs) are a great way to bring your rabbit into new areas but also keep them contained. Pens also make a great place for your rabbit to enjoy special toys and have space to run around and be a bunny.

Grooming

Regular grooming is one of the keys to keeping your rabbit looking and feeling great. I like to schedule monthly grooming sessions with my bunny and have extra coat-brushing in between if my rabbit is shedding or if they have wool fur or just as a way to show extra love.

Brushing: All rabbits shed their coats usually two to three times a year and will benefit from regular brushing to keep extra hairs from floating around their cage. Most of the brushes you find at pet stores that are rabbit-sized will actually be made for cats but should work just fine for your bunny.

Pin brushes (which are made for cats) have a flat base with hundreds of little "pins" attached that come up and run through your rabbit's coat. These brushes work great for short and long haired rabbits and are one of my favorite brushes for every day grooming.

Soft bristled brushes are also a great brush choice for short or rex furred rabbits. These brushed have soft bristles, usually made from nylon or pigs hair, that gently remove extra fur from your rabbit's coat. This kind of brush does not work super-well on long haired rabbits since the bristles stay on the surface of the coat and have trouble really removing mats and tangles.

Long tooth combs, on the other hand, are a great tool for working through and removing tangles. If you have a long haired rabbit, I highly recommend purchasing one of these!

To brush your rabbit: Start at their head and apply soft pressure using long, gentle strokes with the brush. Work your way back towards their tail until you've covered their whole body. You may need to repeat this a few times to remove all the loose fur and hair from their coat.

Most brushes for your rabbit will cost anywhere from a few bucks to $15 and should last you for years. Remember to clean you comb after each use to keep it from accumulating dirt and debris.

Nail Trimming: Rabbits have toe nails that are constantly growing and need to be clipped about every 6 weeks (depending on your rabbit). If you don't keep your rabbit's nails trimmed, you risk a broken nail (which will bleed) or a whole nail being ripped from their foot (which will bleed a lot).

Your rabbit may also have trouble walking properly with long nails and you will be more likely to get scratched when handling your bunny.

You can purchase specialty pet nail clippers (ones made for cats are usually just the right size) or use the big toe nail clippers that are made for us humans, I've found that both work well on rabbits.

Before you start with your rabbit's first nail trimming, recognize that most rabbits will not enjoy having their nails trimmed and may "fight" you on it (by kicking, squirming or giving you the stink-eye during the whole experience).

Once you and your bunny have been through the process a few times you will both become more comfortable with it. If you have a friend or breeder who is experienced with nail trimming, ask them to help you the first couple of times you attempt it. You'll be glad to have their experience and firm hand around.

Here are the things you need to get started:

- o Nail Clipper
- o Corn starch or "Quick Stop" to dab on the nail in case it starts to bleed
- o Paper towel to wipe blood, if needed
- o Friend or helper
- o Chair to sit in
- o Rabbit (I know, that one's obvious)

To trim your rabbit's nails:

1) Start by removing your rabbit from their cage and take them over to the chair or sofa that your helper is sitting in. Set the bunny in the lap of your helper with bunny's head facing away from your helper's body (so bunny's butt should be against your helper's tummy).

2) Pull out a front paw gently away from the body with your hand and look at the nails. There will be five nails on each of the front paws and four on each of the back paws, total of 18 nails to trim.

   The front paws have a thumb-like nail on the inside of each paw (which is called a dew claw). It's easy to miss if you're not looking for it so don't forget to trim that nail too.

3) Look at the first nail on the paw and find the quick. The quick is the line of blood running from the nail bed into the nail and will be a reddish color inside the nail.

   If your rabbit has white nails, this red-section will be very easy to see. If your rabbit has dark nails, you might have to hold a flash light up to the nail to see where the quick starts. Shine the flashlight through the nail and look on the other side to see where the quick blood line is so you know where it is safe to cut.

4) You do not want to cut into the quick (or there will be bleeding) so pick a spot about a quarter inch up the nail away from the quick and clip it off with your nail clippers. Continue around until you've trimmed all the nails on your rabbit.

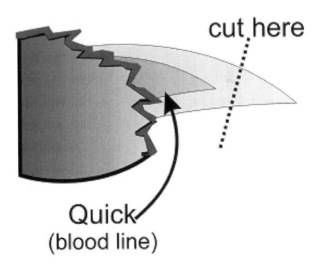

Rabbit Nail

cut here

Quick
(blood line)

If you do accidentally hit the quick, you can dip the nail in the corn starch (or Quick Stop) you pulled out. This will cause the blood to clot faster and stop the bleeding.

Enlist a friend or family member to help the first few times you trim your rabbit's nails. Once you and your rabbit become comfortable with the process, you'll be able to do this on your own. Just take the place of your helper on the couch and place the bunny in your lap before trimming.

And please don't let all this talk of blood scare you away from cutting your rabbit's nails. It is a necessary and important part of bunny grooming.

Most rabbit owners will, at some point, accidentally hit the quick and cause some bleeding. Don't feel bad, but do go slow and take it easy, you'll become very comfortable with this process over time.

Ear Cleaning: You should check and clean your rabbit's ears during grooming sessions. I have a specific time once a week that is "rabbit time" when grooming and cage cleaning happens.

A rabbit's ears serve many purposes, not just to hear. When it's a hot day your rabbit will get rid of extra body heat by dissipating it through their ears. You'll often see them stretch out with their heads up and ears fully opened.

Never try to pick your rabbit up by their ears.
That body part was never made to handle their full body weight and you could break the cartilage inside the ear.

To check your rabbit's ears, hold them in your lap and take one ear into your hand. Open it up gently with your fingers like you would a curling lettuce leaf. Look down inside the ear canal.

If you see any build-up (it usually looks brown and waxy) on the broad part of the ears, you can gentle loosen and wipe it away with a cotton swap dipped in warm water.

Never place the cotton swab (or anything else, for that matter) down into the ear canal – that is an off-limits area and you could cause serious damage by poking around in there.

If you ever notice that your rabbit's inner ears are red, scaly and/or inflamed, then call your vet because your rabbit may have an infection or may have been infested with ear mites.

Ear mites are tiny little parasites that like to burrow into your rabbit's ear canal. If your rabbit ever comes in contact with and starts carrying ear mites, they will often scratch and paw at their ears causing scabs and bleeding. Your vet will be able to prescribe an ointment that will kill the ear mites and help heal your rabbit's ears.

This is another good reason to keep your rabbit indoors because many wild rabbits will spread parasites.

Baths: No baths! Rabbits are very clean animals and do not need to be bathed. It will actually strip their fur of natural oils and can cause itching and scratching.

If your bunny needs a once-over, then try using unscented baby wipes as a quick full body wipe down. You can also find special pet-specific wipes at your local pet store; just make sure the packaging says that they are safe for small animals like rabbits.

Litter Box Training

Rabbits are, by nature, very clean animals and like to keep themselves neat & tidy. Lucky for us, this also carries over into their bathroom habits. Litter box training for a rabbit takes some patience, but rabbits are one of the easiest animals to litter box train (yeah for us!).

Litter box training is great for house rabbits (then they can wander freely without leaving puddles on your rug) and will also cut down dramatically on cage cleaning time since you'll have one main spot to clean up.

Some bunnies will need more time to get the hang of it than others, so always reinforce positive behaviors and never scold or get angry with you rabbit if they mess up and miss the litter box. Accidents happen, but with time and repetition, your rabbit will be running to their litter box nine times out of ten to go to the bathroom.

A rabbit will naturally pick a corner of their cage to "do their business" in and this habit is what makes litter box training so simple for rabbits.

To start you'll need an actual litter box for your rabbit to use.

For Small to Medium-Sized Rabbits:
I like to use corner-shaped litter boxes that fit into the corner of your rabbit's cage because (A) these boxes have two high sides so most urine is easily contained, but the one low side makes it simple for your bunny to jump in and out and (B) they usually have a way to

attach the box onto the cage wall so the box doesn't get knocked over. You can find these at most pet store mega marts and online. Square litter boxes will also work just fine, if you prefer.

For Large to Giant Sized Rabbits:
A normal square-shaped litter box works well if you have a larger sized rabbit. Just make sure that the sides of the litter box are low enough for your rabbit to easily jump in and out of.

Some boxes are made with one wall extra-low so that your rabbit has easy access to the inside. If the side walls of the litter box are too high, your rabbit may knock it over or not use it because it is hard to get into.

Place about an inch or two of absorbent, natural bedding in the bottom of the litter box to soak up moisture and odors.

It's a good idea to attach the litter box to the cage wall, either using clips or wire, so that your rabbit can't knock it over.

Your litter box should be just big enough for your rabbit to hop in and barely turn around. You don't want it to be too big or they might spend all their time in there! Plus, a smaller sized rabbit litter box will take up less space in their cage.

I also don't like to start with a litter box that has a lid. A lot of rabbits will decide that it's a nice place to sleep (looks kind of like a den) and will use it for slumber instead of a litter box.

To begin your bunny training, take your litter box and place it in the corner or area that rabbit normally poops in. This is usually all you need to do to get them to start using it, but if you find that your rabbit doesn't quite get the hint, you can also place a few bits of their poo and some dirty bedding inside the box to help them out.

When you first start litter box training don't clean the box too often. You want it to smell like the place they should go to the bathroom. Once they've started using it on a regular basis you can go to daily cleaning. Until then give it a few days between cleaning, if you can.

Once your rabbit has established that litter box as their chosen place to go to the bathroom then you can pick up the box and move it just about anywhere and they will still use it as their primary bathroom spot.

When placing a litter box around your house start with smaller rooms/spaces and then work up to larger rooms so that your rabbit will get use to running back to their box when they need to use the bathroom.

It will usually take one week to one month for your rabbit to start regularly using a litter box, but if your bunny needs a little more time, be patient. Rabbits that haven't be fixed will also have a tendency to mark their territory and could have more accidents than a rabbit that is spayed or neutered.

Accidents will still happen and your bunny will sometimes not make it to their litter box when they need to relieve themselves. If you notice that your rabbit is missing the litter box often and has started going to the bathroom in a corner somewhere, then try moving the litter box to that corner.

When your rabbit does have an accident in the house be sure to clean the area with an odor neutralizing spray (which you can get from a pet store) so that the spot doesn't smell like a bathroom place.

If the problem still continues, you may have given your bunny too much space too quickly. Take them down to a smaller space with their litter box (a play pen or baby fence works great for this in the house) and then slowly work up to larger spaces over the next few weeks.

You may also want to place several litter boxes around the house if you allow your rabbit full run so that they have somewhere close by to go to the bathroom.

What to do if Your Rabbit Bites

One of the biggest fears of any pet rabbit owner is that

their rabbit will bite. Those furry bunnies have some big teeth and a bite will hurt and usually draw blood.

Most rabbits that are brought up with people from a young age don't have a tendency to bite and will only do so when they feel threatened or scared. This is one of the reasons it so important to pick a rabbit that's calm and socialized from the very beginning and leave difficult rabbits in the hands of more experienced rabbit owners.

Even with a calm rabbit, you may still have a bunny that bites. This is usually done for a couple of reasons:

1) Being Scared or Fearful

2) Showing Dominance

3) Food Biting

Being Scared or Fearful

This is the most common reason for a rabbit to bite. When introducing new people to your bunny be sure that they know the proper way to pet and interact with your rabbit.

A rabbit that has been dropped many times or treated roughly will often bite as a way to escape those circumstances. They've learned that if they bite they get to go back to their safe cage.

Always try to be calm and gentle when handling your rabbit. If you or your bunny are getting worked up, then take a time out for you both to calm down before beginning again. With time and repetition your rabbit will realize that you are not going to hurt them.

Sometimes a rabbit will also nip to let you know they've had enough and are ready to go back to their cage or be put down. Keep an eye out for the body language your rabbit uses during these times and stop the play before they've had enough.

Showing Dominance

Rabbits live in a hierarchical society, just like dogs, meaning that there is always a bunny who is "in charge" of the group. If you've ended up with a bunny that shows an aggressive and dominant nature, then you've got to establish that you are the boss.

These behaviors could include things like nipping or biting you when they want you to move, give them a treat or even when you're just sitting there together on the couch.

It's very important that you don't give in at these

moments and do whatever your rabbit wants. That will only increase and solidify their behavior.

When your rabbit exhibits these behavior, be firm but gentle and move them back to the position they were in before they started showing aggression or remove them from the couch (or area you're at) and claim the space as your own.

It may sound silly, but I find that if I say out loud, "I'm in charge here Mister and this is my couch" in a firm voice that I act more authoritative towards my bunny.

Rabbits, like all animals, can read our body language and sometimes need to see that we have confidence in ourselves and that we believe that we are the ones in charge.

If all else fails, then take your bunny back to their cage for a "time out" so they know that you control their space.

Food Biting

Some rabbits will accidentally nip you when eating treats from your hand (which is no big deal, it was an accident) but some will be aggressive around food and lunge or come at you whenever food is around.

The first thing to recognize is that this is normal behavior for a more dominant rabbit. In the wild they would establish that they are the bunny in charge and, therefore, they get to eat first.

Once again, we need to establish that we are in charge (like with dominance biting) but also take the time to train our rabbit to eat calmly around us.

Start by feeding your rabbit outside of their cage since they tend to look at the cage as "their space." Go to more neutral territory, like the living room floor. Take your rabbit's food bowl or a treat and place it in front of you with your hand over it (or a basket if you're worried about your hand getting bit).

Allow your rabbit to smell the food but not eat it. You're basically saying to your bunny, "Yes, there is food here , it's mine." After ten to fifteen seconds, remove your hand from the food and allow your bunny to start munching.

If you're feeding treats from your hand, start with something long (like a piece of hay or a long green leaf) to give you some distance from their teeth.

If, at any point, your rabbit starts to become aggressive, then move them away from the food and claim it yourself by holding it away or placing your hand (or basket) on top of it.

Repeating this process over a few days to a few weeks will train your rabbit to realize that you give food and you take it away, that you are in control.

Inside their cage you can also experiment with placing the food in different locations so that your rabbit will never know exactly where to expect it. This variation makes it harder for your bunny to be territorial and dominant around the food because they are never sure where and when it will be coming.

Moving Your Bunny

At some point or another you'll find that you need to move and travel with your rabbit. This is usually as simple as a trip to the vet's office but may involve moving to a new house (so your bunny is in limbo for a day or two during moving) and other similar events.

Rabbits prefer not to be moved around a lot. It can cause quite a bit of stress to build up so choose your travels carefully and keep your rabbit's best interests at heart.

When you do need to transport your bunny from one location to another, I recommend that this be done in a separate transport carrying cage.

Your rabbit's normal cage is probably too large to be easily moved around and is full of his bunny stuff. A transport cage is a smaller enclosure that just serves as temporary living quarters so it doesn't need to be as grand.

My favorite carrying cages are wire construction (wire walls and top) with a plastic or metal tray at the bottom. These kinds of cages usually have a top-opening door that makes it super easy to lift you rabbit in and out of the cage. They also have a deep tray to keep bedding in the cage and not all over your car. I also like these cages because a small food and water dish can be easily attached to the side of the cage if you're going to be out with your rabbit for more than a few hours.

Wire cages also have great ventilation and don't get hot and stinky like plastic transport cages can.

If you don't end up going with a wire carrying cage, then you can find small plastic cat transport cages at most pet stores that will work in a pinch. The doors usually open from the front, which makes it more difficult to remove your bunny and bedding tends to get rather messy because this cage wasn't designed to hold it in place.

Wire transport cages are very easy to make yourself! If you're interested, you can download free plans at our website www.EverythingRabbit.com

Next, we're going to focus on keeping your pet clean and healthy by going over a chores checklist, vet visits, what to watch out for during illness and some great tips to help your rabbit live a long, healthy life.

Sarah Martin

Chapter 8:

My Bunny's Health & Wellness

In this chapter we're going to talk about keeping your rabbit healthy! A chores check list is an important part of any rabbit-care routine. See below for a list of daily, weekly, monthly, and yearly things that your bunny will need.

I use a checklist all the time for younger rabbit owners. Most parents print a copy every week, have the kids check off the list as they do the chores, and then turn them in on Sundays. Easy peasy!

Chores Check List

- o Daily – Remove any uneaten food, treats, or debris. Add new hay, greens, and pellets.

- o Daily – Clean water bottle or bowl and refill with clean, fresh water.

- o Daily - Check that cage and litter box don't need spot cleaning in an area that has gotten soggy or dirty. Check that all toys are in good condition.

- o Daily – Observe your rabbit for signs of illness.

- o Daily – Play with and pet your bunny.

- o Weekly – Cage and litter box cleaning, replacing bedding. Thoroughly wash and clean food, hay, and water containers.

- o Weekly – Brushing (as needed).

- o Monthly – Grooming and nail trimming (this may be more often if your rabbit has wool fur or is shedding).

- o Monthly - Health Checks (done by you).

- o Yearly - Health Checks (done by your veterinarian).

Below is a single-page version of the Chores Checklist if you want copies. You can also print a copy of the chores PDF at our website www.EverythingRabbit.com.

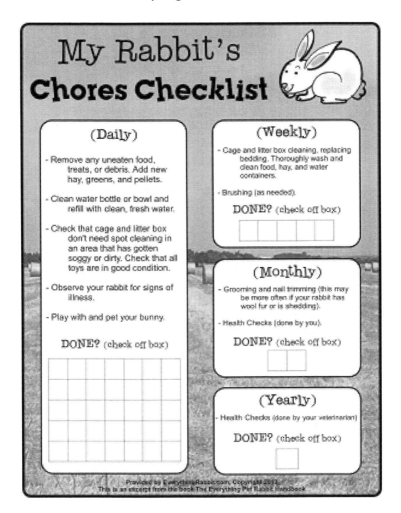

Vet Visits and Spay or Neutering

Finding a good veterinarian will be one of the first things that you'll need to do as a bunny parent.

If you need to have your rabbit spayed or neutered, you'll also want to find a vet who can perform that procedure for you.

When searching for a vet, my favorite method to find a reliable vet is through recommendations. Ask whoever you purchased your rabbit from if they know a good vet. If they don't, ask them if they know someone else who might. It's always great to have a firsthand account from someone who's worked with a vet and had a great experience.

If you end up hunting on your own, then start by looking up vets in your area that list "rabbits" and one of their animals. Often times they may just list "exotic animals" under their specialties and rabbits often fall under that. (Isn't it nice to know you're an exotic pet owner now?)

Once you find a vet that treats rabbits, do some research online and see how their other patient experiences have been. You can also ask the vet's office for a list of references and call to check them out.

Ask if they offer free consultations or tours so you can meet the staff and the vet before making your decision.

When you make your first appointment with your new vet make sure that they are comfortable working with rabbits and have a lot of past rabbit experience.

Look Around:
Don't be afraid to look around and find a vet that is a good fit for you and your bunny. This person will be a very important part of your rabbit's life so you want to be certain and comfortable with your selection.

If you live in the United States or Canada:
Right now (at the time of writing this) in the USA, there are no required vaccinations for rabbits so your bunny will not need yearly shots.

If you live in the United Kingdom:
It is currently recommended that you have your rabbit vaccinated for Myxomatosis and Viral Haemorrhagic. If you ever plan on boarding your pet, these are often required by the boarding facility.

Always check with your vet to see what is recommended for your rabbit's health and wellness.

Help Your Rabbit Live a Longer and Fuller Life

You can help your rabbit live a happy and long life by providing him with a healthy, stimulating environment. Below are just a few of the things you can do on a regular basis to engage with your pet.

Give Your Rabbit:

- o   Regular exercise (exercise pens work great for this).

- o   Greens and hay in their diet.

- o   Life indoors (on average an indoor rabbit will live twice as long as outdoor rabbits).

- o Regular vet visits and monthly health checks (monthly checks done by you).

- o Socialization and engagement (love your bunny and spend time with them).

Monitoring Health

Along with performing monthly health checks and yearly vet visits you should constantly be monitoring your pet, every day, for signs of illness.

Most rabbits will give off signals through body language or behavior which tell you they are not feeling well. Here are just a few of the signs to watch out for.

Signs of Illness:

- o Lethargic or slow movement with delayed reaction time.

- o Hunched over or tucked in on themselves in a corner of the cage with that, "I'm sick, get away from me" look in their eyes.

- o Not eating/drinking or decreased levels of food and water consumption.

- o Weight loss.

- o Looking like they are in pain or that moving is causing them pain.

- o Severe diarrhea or changes in droppings and/or urine.

- o Slobbering at the mouth or discharge from nose and/or eyes.

- o Ragged looking with unkempt fur. Flakey patches or crusty bald spots.

- o Any type of sore or wound on the body. Often you'll be able feel lumps or hot spots, but the abscess may not be visible.

This is not a comprehensive list and, if you're interested, I recommend finding a book on rabbit illness and disease to read up on the many signs to watch out.

Most importantly, trust your gut! You know your rabbit better than anyone else and if something doesn't feel right or look right, then pay attention. It could be your internal system noticing something that your logical brain missed.

You know how you've felt like something wasn't right before and it turned out to be true? Well, keep that sense in mind when working with your rabbit. If you think they are sick and might need medical attention, then go ahead and take action.

Sarah Martin

Chapter 9:

Getting Involved

Now that you've got a good grasp on rabbit basics, it's time to think about where to go from here.

The world of rabbits is full of wonderful and loving people who truly care about their pets. Welcome to the club!

But don't stop here – there are many ways for you to continue to interact with rabbit lovers and build your base of bunny knowledge. The more you know, the better pet owner you'll be and you'll continue to have a great experience of owning a rabbit.

Here are just a few suggestions of ways to keep up with the rabbit habit...

Clubs

There are more rabbit clubs all over the place (seriously, they're everywhere) and you probably have at least one or two in your area.

Here are some of the big ones that you can join or check out to find more info on smaller clubs:

American Rabbit Breeders Association

Website: www.ARBA.net

The British Rabbit Council

Website: www.thebrc.org

The Dominion Rabbit & Cavy Breeders Association (Canadian based)

Website: www.drcba.ca

Australian National Rabbit Council Inc.

Website: www.AustralianNationalRabbitCouncil.com

Local 4-H and FFA clubs are also great for kids under age 18. They usually have groups that meet once or twice a month and focus on rabbit handling and education.

You can look them up through www.4-H.org and

www.FFA.org

Charities

There are many local, regional, and international rabbit charities and shelters that need support from rabbit lovers.

One of my favorites, The House Rabbit Society, is a non-profit volunteer-run club that has a great website: www.rabbit.org

Forums

There are online forums everywhere to discuss any topic you could image and rabbits are no exception. I've found forums to be great ways to connect with other rabbit owners and get questions answered on just about any rabbit-related topic.

Continuing Education

I know that you're a reader and want to be a good rabbit owner (since you've already gone through this book).

You should know that your journey doesn't stop here but has only begun. Continue to build your base of rabbit knowledge, even if it's only a little bit of reading every week.

That time, built up over the years that you will have your bunny, will slowly make you an expert and a terrific pet owner!

There are 100s of books on all sorts of bunny-related subjects. Rabbit-related video training and seminars are also a great source of information.

Newsletters can keep you up to date on what's new and important in the rabbit world and a magazine or two on rabbits is a fun way to learn about bunny-related things.

When you have time, please also check out our website www.EverythingRabbit.com. We've loaded it up with free info and downloads so you can find out great bits of bunny info!

Don't forget that you are now the most important person in your rabbit's life. Their care, happiness, and love depends on you. Luckily, you already know that you're going to be a GREAT bunny owner and have a wonderful and fulfilling relationship with your rabbit because you've taken the steps to learn more about your furry friend.

Enjoy the time with your rabbit and give him all the love and attention he (or she) needs to live a happy life.

Sarah Martin

Closing Thoughts

If you ever have any questions, I'd be happy to hear from you. Please feel free to email me at Sarah@EverythingRabbit.com

While you're online, please take a moment to visit our website and become part of our rabbit community! You can see us on the web at www.EverythingRabbit.com. I always look forward to hearing from readers and would love to get stories and photos of your new bunny!

While you're there, feel free to check out our amazing newsletter and free downloads that come with this book (like plans to make your own carrying cage, a copy of the monthly heath checklist and the chores checklist).

We'd love to have you sign up and stay connected with us. It's only through your support that we are able to provide all the information on our site for free.

Thank you for purchasing this book! **We'd love it if you would leave a** review on Amazon**, it really does help out!** A portion of our proceeds go towards supporting free rabbit education and 4-H clubs.

We are here to support and encourage every rabbit owner so that you and your bunny can enjoy quality time together.

Once again, thank you for taking the time to read my book and for taking the first steps towards becoming a knowledgeable & experienced rabbit owner. It is my pleasure to be able to provide you with this information, collected from years of hands-on experience and through the advice of countless experts in the rabbit world.

P.S. Keep an eye out for our next book and instructional videos on rabbit handling, behavior and training!

P.P.S. If you are a rabbit breeder (or just interested in rabbit breeding), then check out our book: *How to Breed a Rabbit* on Amazon.

About the Author

Sarah Martin is the founder of the rabbit authority website www.EverythingRabbit.com and the author of several top books on rabbits and rabbit care.

A Note From Sarah: My first bunny love started over 20 years ago when a little bundle of fur with big, floppy ears entered my life. I would never be the same again.

I started writing and interviewing top experts from all over the rabbit world (and my own personal experiences as a rabbit breeder/owner) so that other rabbit lovers, like myself, could have somewhere to gather and find great information on EVERYTHING related to rabbits and bunnies.

All of my books are created as an in-depth guide to help newbie and advanced rabbit people alike expand their knowledge, have fun with their rabbits, and avoid major pitfalls along the way.

This lead me to create www.EverythingRabbit.com , a place to get all your questions answered, to find cool tips and fun activities, and to build a community of people who love rabbits as much as I do.

Wishing you and your furry friends many blessings!

Sarah Martin

Thank you for purchasing our book.

If you enjoyed this publication please don't forget to leave a review on Amazon so that we can make our future revisions even better! It helps us out in so many ways ☺

ATTN TEACHERS: If you are a kid's club 4-H leader, FFA leader, or home school instructor and would like to receive training material for your group, please email me. I'm happy to help!

Made in the USA
San Bernardino, CA
09 December 2014